The Red Tempest

Dave Wright

Dave Wright

DEDICATION

I dedicate this book to my wife, Sue, who is my first draft editor and who is a continual source of encouragement.

CONTENTS

Chapter 1
The Empire Builder

The westbound Empire Builder rolled across the snow-covered grasslands of Montana when a buxom redhead wearing a loose-fitting floral dress burst through the sliding door of the dining car. She swayed from one foot to the other as she staggered down the aisle.

"Eh! This table six?" she said in a voice that could be heard throughout the car.

"Yes," said a man who was one of three passengers already seated at the table. "Must be here for the 6:30 seating." He was medium height—five-eight or five-nine—and had dark curly hair. He wore pressed blue jeans and a burgundy turtleneck with the logo, *Henderson Accounting* on his chest. The man had been preoccupied with checking his fingernails but looked up and gestured to the empty seat across from him. "Help yourself."

"Don't mind if I do," said the woman as she plopped into the seat. She carried a massive carpet bag with a paisley print. It jingled with the sound of clinking glass when she dropped it on the floor next to her. She shook her curls as if to clear her head. "Ah. That's better."

A waiter approached their table. "May I take your beverage orders?"

"Coors and a 7-Up," said the redhead immediately. She turned to the woman next to her who had been pecking at her cell phone. "How 'bout you, sweetheart?"

The woman wore a somber face and a prim business suit. She appeared mildly inconvenienced at the interruption. "Coffee," she said. "Black…unless it's awful."

"You can decide for yourself," said the waiter. "I'll bring the cream if you need it."

The oval-faced woman swept her bangs from her eyes, glanced once more at her phone, and turned her attention to the middle-aged couple who sat across from her.

The waiter followed her gaze. "And for you?" he asked.

"Red wine for both of us," said the man.

"No, Max," said the tight-faced woman sitting next to him. She wore Spandex leggings, a tight-fitting blouse, and looked like she had just emerged from a workout.

"I'll have a Chardonnay." She twirled her ropey blond hair with her left hand and rolled her fingers on the table with the other. "After thirty years, you should know that."

The man gave her a bewildered expression. "Since when did that change? You always have red wine at home."

"Remember? I always drink white when I travel. Red upsets my stomach." The woman looked up at the waiter and repeated, "White, please."

When the waiter moved to the next table, the redhead reached across the table exposing her freckled cleavage to the curly-headed man. "Hi there, handsome. I'm Maggie McFinnigan. How ya doin'?"

"Fine. Thanks," he said, standing over the table to shake her hand. He quickly lifted his gaze from the woman's bosom. "I'm Max Wharton, and this is my wife, Linda."

"Nice to meet ya," said Maggie and turned again to the small woman seated next to her. "And you?"

"I'm Beth Lancer," said the woman. She extended a reluctant handshake.

"Where ya all headed, then?" said Maggie turning to the couple.

"We're getting off at Whitefish—skiing at the Whitefish Mountain Resort," said Max. Then, turning to Linda he added, "Supposed to be celebrating thirty years of bliss."

Linda rolled her eyes. "Bliss might be an overstatement," she said as she poked Max in his belly and chuckled, "but the exercise ought to do him good, don't you think?"

"He looks pretty good to me," said Maggie with a wink in his direction. "How about you, little one?" she said as she turned to Beth. "Where you headin'?"

Beth glanced at Maggie and then at her coffee cup. "I'm going to Seattle—thinking of opening a bookstore. I hear Seattle has a lot of them."

"A bookstore!" shouted Maggie. "I love books—'specially those trashy romance novels." She pulled her musical handbag from the floor and set it on her lap. Then she extracted a pack of breath mints and a crushed bag of Doritos before laying her prize on the table—*The Romance of Lady Candue*. "It's the first in a series," boasted Maggie. "Author by the name of Lance Freeport. He's a heck of a writer. I've got the rest of 'em in my cabin. Can't wait to read 'em all." She held it up and showed it to Beth. A bare-legged woman wearing a strategically placed boa filled the cover. "Ever heard of it?"

Beth glanced quickly at the book, her face coloring, "No. I'm afraid not."

"If you're gonna open a bookstore, better make sure it's in stock," said Maggie. "From what I've read so far, it'll be a best seller."

The waiter delivered their beverages. As soon as he left the table, Maggie took a large sip of 7-Up. After rattling around in her handbag, she produced a single-shot bottle of Seagram's Seven. She smiled as she unscrewed the cap. "Bought a sampler supply of these mini shooters before I left home. Got plenty more in my suitcase. Anybody care for a shot before dinner?" She raised her glass. "Never know when the bar might be closed."

"No thanks," said Beth as she caressed her coffee cup. The others raised their wine glasses to a chorus of "cheers."

"Must be planning on a long trip if you had to stock up," observed Max. "Where are *you* headed?"

"Alaska!" bellowed Maggie.

"And, why Alaska?" asked Linda.

"Why, for the men, of course!"

The couple laughed and lifted their glasses to another toast. "For the men."

Beth put her hand to her mouth, suppressing her first smile of the evening, but added her cup to the toast.

"What kind of man are you looking for?" asked Max.

"Sure as hell ain't gonna be the kind I left in Two Harbors. Got hooked up right out of high school with a good-for-nuthin' beanpole of a man. Look," she said as she sat up in her seat and spread her arms. "The poor bugger was no match for me—plenty of sex but no love." She took a long drink from her Seven-Seven. "No romance. Always felt kinda' like a quick stab in the dark."

Linda smiled. "You're married?"

"Was—for about three years," said Maggie. "I was Pa's last hope. My two older sisters—they flew the coop before they got stuck at *Finney's Fish Market* for the rest a their lives."

"Your father owns *Finney's Fish Market*?" asked Max. "We used to stop there and pick up smoked fish every time we went up the North Shore. Clyde loved it."

"That's the one," said Maggie.

4

"Clyde," reflected Max. "He's our only son. We're empty nesters now. At least I think we are. He moved out a few years ago. Then he showed up at the door offering to babysit the house while we were going to be gone." Max looked at his wife and added, "Hope he hasn't turned into a full-time squatter by the time we get home."

"You're always down on Clyde," said Linda. "He's a good boy. He's just taken a while to launch.

"He's not a boy anymore, Linda. For God's sake, he's twenty-nine years old." Max took a gulp of wine and stole a glance at an attractive woman seated across the aisle.

Linda delivered an accusing stare to the back of his head. "You were supposed to plan a trip to the North Shore last summer. Remember? It would have been good for Clyde."

"You know as well as I do that Clyde wouldn't have come along. And besides, there's too many bugs that time of year." Max shrugged, checked his nails, and looked into the window. "But I *did* plan this trip."

"Big deal," said Linda. "We take a trip here every March." She looked across the table. "But we usually don't ski together. Our therapist says it's good for us to have a little time apart."

"You get plenty of time to yourself," said Max turning back to the table. "You spend half your life at the club: women's jazzercise, women's body building classes, women's Zumba class, sunbathing for hours under a heat lamp that looks like a coffin." Max took another sip of wine before adding, "And the other half at the casino."

"But I win more than I lose," said Linda to the other travelers.

"You need to check your math, Linda," said Max. He turned his attention to the table. "Sorry. Too much information."

Linda turned to Maggie. "Don't mind him. Tell me about your sisters. Sounds like they didn't like the fish market."

"My sisters hated it," said Maggie. "We all smelled like smoked fish: salmon, whitefish, lake trout—even smelt. You name it, we smoked it. I don't mind fish. I just didn't like the family business." She set the Seven-Seven on the table and took up her bottle of Coors. "Pop had visions of keeping the business in the McFinnigan family—would a been a lot easier if he'd had the son he wanted." She laughed. "But he was cursed with three daughters: My oldest sister, Val ran off to Canada with a hedge fund manager…and last we heard from Brenda, my middle sister, she was hitchhiking through Mexico with some guy who had just stepped off the Superior Hiking Trail."

Beth had taken a sudden interest in the conversation. "This is beginning to sound like a Victorian tragedy," she said in a voice loud enough to be heard. "So that left you, the youngest to take over the family business?"

Maggie nodded to Beth. "You got it, sister. It gets better. Ridley—that's my ex—had his eye on *Finney's Fish Market* since we were in high school together. Pop loved him—hired him when he was sixteen, and Ridley never left. He was sweet to me—kinda' like a brother. Pop was happy when he proposed." Maggie took a sip of beer. "After lookin' over the pickens in Two Harbors I thought, 'Things could be worse than Ridley'—so I said yes. Soon after the wedding, Pop started badgering me about wantin' a grandson—and Ridley was more'n happy to tell him he was tryin' his best."

"I take it you didn't get pregnant?" said Beth.

"Nope." Maggie looked out the window as the train rolled into Shelby, Montana. "Ridley blamed the beer. He used to say, 'I told you that beer and babies don't mix.'"

Maggie swirled her bottle. "Ridley was probably right, but I think it's me and motherhood that don't mix…and if I got pregnant, what if it wasn't a boy?"

She set down her bottle of Coors and leaned across the table to confide to the women, "I paid cash for my regular trips to Lake View Pharmacy. Men are so dense."

"They certainly are," said Linda as she glanced at Max.

Max ignored her comment while Maggie continued, "Poor Ridley kept on tryin'. What a pounding—I felt like a brood mare in heat," she laughed, "but I made the most of it. When I didn't get pregnant for a year, Ridley kept askin', 'What's wrong with you? Maybe you should get tested.' I just smiled and said, 'I'm doin' my part, hon. The little fellas just don't wanna take. Maybe it's you, Ridley.'"

Maggie sipped her Seven-Seven. "Ridley was too proud to get himself tested." She winked at Beth, "or was too frightened about what they might find."

The waiter arrived with a tray of food balanced on his arm. "Who had the vegetarian special?"

"I did," said Linda.

"And the cod?"

Beth raised her hand.

"And the steaks?"

"The rare one's mine," said Maggie.

"And I ordered the medium," said Max.

"Will there be anything else?" asked the waiter.

"How about a little extra butter?" said Max.

Maggie smiled. "A little extra sour cream for me."

Linda looked at Max's plate and scowled. "You could have at least ordered the fish."

"We're on vacation," said Max as he cut into his baked potato and slathered it with butter and sour cream. He turned to Maggie. "So, the family gave up on you because you didn't get pregnant?"

"*I* gave up on the family," said Maggie as she held a juicy bite of sirloin on her fork and pointed it at Max. "Made it a lot easier to leave Two Harbors when they gave up on me too."

"You think you'll find the man you want in Alaska?" asked Linda.

Maggie put the morsel in her mouth and chewed reflectively. "Don't know what I'll find in Alaska, but I know fish." Then she pointed to her paperback with her fork. "And the more I read this stuff, the more I learn 'bout men." She swallowed and said, "From what I hear, Alaska has lotsa both."

Linda looked at Beth who was picking at her food and pecking at her phone. "What's so interesting on your phone?"

Beth blushed again and quickly returned her phone to her purse. She thought for a moment, then replied, "Note to my cat sitter. I have two cats."

Maggie rolled her eyes.

Linda asked, "What are their names?"

"I'm a librarian," said Beth, "so ah...I picked names from literature. My calico is Emily—after Emily Dickinson."

"I suppose the other one is Waldo—after Ralph Waldo Emerson?" laughed Linda.

"No. It's Thor," said Beth decisively.

"Thor!" shouted Maggie. "I can see you having a cat named Emily, but I can't imagine a Thor in your life—a cat or any other creature."

"After Henry David *Thor*eau," said Beth quietly.

"Didn't know that was his nickname," said Maggie.

The waiter returned and asked if anyone wanted dessert. "We have a chocolate torte, orange Sherbert, or a fresh fruit dish."

Beth ordered the Sherbert; Maggie and Max had the torte; Linda scowled at Max and ordered the fresh fruit. "Is it organic?" She demanded of the waiter.

"I'm sure it is," said the waiter. "The strawberries are too small to be anything but."

Chapter 2
The Empire Builder

Max

Max was the first to leave the diner. He nodded to Linda and the rest of the group. "I'm going to take a walk," he said. "Linda thinks a little exercise will do me good." He made his way past the cabin he shared with Linda, strolled through both sleeper cars, and went directly to the bar below the dome car. He ordered a Budweiser and found a table in the corner where he laid out a game of solitaire.

I wonder what my life would have been like if Linda hadn't gotten pregnant the first month we met—more freedom and less responsibility, I suppose...Maybe there's still time for that. I've accumulated enough money—thanks to those bonuses from Axel and Sons—but with the latest change in the law, Linda is bound to find out about it.

Max chewed a fingernail and flipped over an ace to start a new row when his cell phone rang. He recognized the caller. *Thank God.*

Frankie Hillsborough was one of Max's college classmates. They had attended the University of Minnesota and Carlson School of Business. Max had gotten a Master of Accountancy and his CPA. Frankie had gotten an MBA and continued on to law school at the University of Chicago. While Max was intelligent, Frankie was brilliant. After working on Wall Street for several years as a successful investment broker, he became a criminal defense attorney specializing in clients accused of tax evasion. Frankie was one of the few people Max could trust with his delicate situation.

Max tapped his phone. "Frankie. Thanks for returning my call."

"No problem. I saw that you have another deposit from Axel and Sons."

"That's right. I finished their return before I left on vacation. They can't believe I can find more creative ways to minimize their taxes."

"You're certainly a golden boy in their eyes," laughed Frankie. "Bonuses of fifty grand a year for the last ten years? That's adding up to some big money."

"I can't believe it myself," said Max. "I got the *Axel and Sons* account when they were a startup pharmaceutical company. One of their new drugs came on the market, and it was like hitting the jackpot. When I saved them five million dollars in taxes that first year, Mr. Axel called me and offered me a position. When I told him I couldn't accept because of a non-compete clause I had signed with *Henderson Accounting*, he offered me a generous cash bonus with the stipulation that *Henderson* continue to assign me to their account."

"Pretty appreciative," said Frankie, "but there's a new law that's cracking down on foreign bank accounts."

"I read about it," said Max. "It's called FATCA, right? The Foreign Account Tax Compliance Act?"

"Correct. It's going to throw a wrench into our system of depositing those bonuses into a Swiss bank account. In the past, Switzerland was not required to share that information with the IRS, but now the government may find out that you haven't been reporting that income."

"I'm less worried about the government finding out about my little nest egg than I am about Linda finding out about it. She'd have it spent or gambled away in less than a year."

Max ran a hand through his hair. "Will I go to jail?"

"There may be a way to avoid all that," said Frankie. "If you file an offshore voluntary disclosure before the government audits you or begins a criminal tax investigation, you might get by with only paying the back taxes, interest, and penalties—hopefully, no jail time."

"I don't want to go to jail," said Max as he studied his fingernails. "How is the account doing? Last I checked, it appeared that your investment expertise has paid off."

Frankie chuckled again. "Thanks. I've been happy with the returns, too. You've always been frugal, Max. I think if you wanted to come clean, pay me, and pay the taxes, you'd still have a pretty substantial nest egg."

"I'd be happy to pay the taxes, but there'll be hell to pay when Linda sees next year's tax return. She'll find out how wealthy we really are, and I'll never get rid of her."

"Sorry, Max. I'm a criminal tax attorney, not a divorce lawyer."

"I know," sighed Max. "Start the paperwork for the voluntary disclosure. Keep in touch."

He placed the phone on the table and gulped a couple of Tums.

It's time to say some goodbyes, thought Max. *Goodbye to Linda. Goodbye to Clyde. Goodbye to Axel and Sons. Goodbye to Henderson Accounting. Goodbye to Minnesota. I'm sick of it all.*

He took a sip of Budweiser and returned to his game of solitaire.

Beth

Beth returned to the sleeper car and smiled for the second time that evening.

Cats, thought Beth. *I hate cats—ever since I was a kennel attendant at the vet clinic during high school. Found out I'm allergic to the darn things—had to wash down two Claritin with a double espresso at Caribou Coffee before I went to work—got so jittery I could barely fill a water bowl.*

Her thoughts returned to her dinner conversation. *Those people didn't need to see that I was jotting notes about them on my phone. It's a writer's habit.* She laughed out loud. *Thor—after Henry David Thoreau. That was a good one—more like the god of wishful thinking.*

She pulled the temporary desk from the wall in her compartment and opened her laptop.

Maybe I'm wasting my life in St. Paul. I need inspiration for my writing—and adventure for my life. That crazy Maggie might be on to something.

The first page of *Lady Candue Meets Her Match* by Lance Freeport flashed onto her screen.

Lady Candue needs a hero like Thor, thought Beth. *I like it—the Norse god of thunder—but someone like Thor would never frequent a Seattle bookstore. Maybe I should look for my character in Alaska.*

She let her imagination wander as she tapped out the opening scene for her eighth and final book in the series.

Linda

Linda passed Beth's compartment, entered the next car, and stopped outside the door to their deluxe sleeper. As she fumbled for her key, she noticed her reflection in its window.

I should have ordered the salad, she thought. Why in the world would the cod come breaded and deep fried? Maybe some calisthenics here in the hallway.

She looked again at her profile outlined in spandex.

Not bad, really. I hope Clint liked the pictures. What was the name of that bar where we agreed to meet? Ah yes. That was it. The Blind Bandit.

Maggie

Maggie returned to her sleeper and pulled out a peppermint schnapps mini shooter. She removed the cap, emptied the bottle, and opened her Alaskan atlas.

Homer. I heard that's a fishing port. It ought to be a place that has plenty of men looking for a sturdy woman.

She crawled into her bunk and fell into a deep sleep.

Chapter 3
Whitefish, Montana

Max

The Empire Builder pulled into the Whitefish train station at 10:30 pm—only a half hour late. Max had remained in the dome car until shortly before ten when he stopped by their sleeper to pack his duffel bag and to pull his ski coat from the storage closet.

Linda was seated watching the moonlit mountains. Her packed suitcase was next to her.

Max cleared his throat to get her attention. "Linda, you're always looking for more time to yourself," said Max. "We've always skied separately on our vacations but what do you think about staying at different places too?"

Linda gave him a surprised look. "I suppose…" she said slowly, "that might be okay. When did you decide this?"

"After winning a half dozen games of solitaire, I thought it was a sign."

"And you accuse me of having a gambling problem," chuckled Linda. "Who gets the Lodge at Whitefish Lake—the one we reserved?"

"You can have that one," said Max. "I've booked a room at the Hampton Inn…but I expect it's only fair that we pay our own expenses."

Linda frowned, "You already booked a place? Must have been pretty sure I'd agree…But the lodge is three-fifty a night."

"You can cancel and rebook if you like. The Hampton is half that. Of course, you were the one who wanted to reserve the plush accommodations—and with the hundred grand that you inherited from your parents, you can do as you like."

Linda considered Max's suggestion for only a moment. "I think that's a great idea—may not have been what our therapist had in mind, but it might be the best thing for our marriage."

"I thought you might agree," said Max. "Enjoy your vacation."

Max proceeded down the stairs, gathered his skis, boots, and poles, and stepped off the train as soon as the conductor opened the door. He took a deep breath of clean mountain air and hoisted his skis on his shoulder. *Time to clear my head—no henpecking for two weeks.*

The *Bulldog Saloon* greeted him a block south of the station. He had forgotten to relieve himself before he left the train, so he dropped his gear at the door and stepped into the restroom. *Look at this place,* he marveled. *Gambling, porn on the walls, and no partition between the toilets and the urinals. Perfect for a gambling-addicted exhibitionist. Linda would love it.*

He passed the slot machines, left the *Bulldog Saloon,* and hiked south on the sidewalk to his new accommodations. Every step felt lighter.

Linda

"What luck!" said Linda to herself as soon as Max left her alone in the sleeper car. *Two weeks to myself.* She opened her phone and texted Clint. "U won't believe it. Got the suite at the Whitefish Lake Lodge all to myself. U at *The Blind Bandit?*"

A moment later her phone lit up with a thumbs up. "All yours, babe. Meet u at our corner table."

Linda felt a tingle of excitement as she stepped off the train and flagged a taxi. "The Whitefish Lake Lodge, please," she said. "Can you wait a moment for me to check in? Then I'd like a ride to *The Blind Bandit.*"

Linda stood at the desk at *Whitefish Lodge.*

"May I have a credit card and I.D., please?" said the receptionist.

"Sure." Linda opened her purse and flipped through a collection of credit cards in her wallet—*Chase Manhattan, maxed out. Wells Fargo, maxed out, Capital One, maxed out.*

"Here, I made a payment on this one," she said, as she handed a Discover card to the receptionist. She drummed her fingers on the counter as she waited.

"I'm sorry, ma'am. This one won't go through."

"Damn. Oh, sorry. My check must have crossed in the mail. Try this one. It's new." She slid a PayPal Mastercard across the desk.

"Thank you," smiled the receptionist. "How many key cards?"

"Two, please."

"You're in room 403. It's a beauty. The balcony overlooks the mountain."

Linda thanked the woman. As she hurried to the room to change clothes, she contemplated her financial situation. *I could pay off all my credit cards with the money from my parents' estate, but I wouldn't have much left. Maybe I need a trip to Vegas.*

Most of the patrons had left for the night, but Clint was waiting patiently at a corner table nursing a Black Butte Porter. Linda peered into the low-lit bar. His long legs stretched from under the table. A dun-colored cowboy hat perched at an angle over his windblown complexion. Wisps of grey-flecked auburn hair escaped from under the hat. A Montecristo cigar peeped out of the breast pocket of his western-cut shirt. His Sam Elliot mustache draped over a perfect set of teeth that appeared when he saw her.

"Yer a sight for sore eyes," said Clint as he rose to meet her. "Been a long year. Didn't know if you'd remember."

"How could I forget?" said Linda, blushing slightly. "It's our annual get-together. Did you get my pictures?"

"Sho' did—kept the memory alive. Look at 'em most every night. You look great."

"I'm trying to stay in shape," said Linda as she smoothed her skimpy skirt over black leggings, "but I think age is catching up to me."

Clint took a long appraising look. "Lookin' pretty damn good if ya ask me. What do ya say we have a drink…then renew our friendship?"

How nice. Max never compliments me on my looks—or anything else for that matter.

Clint pointed to the seat next to him. "So, you got a room to yourself? Where's Max?"

"He wanted to stay by himself," shrugged Linda as she slid into the booth, "but that'll make our visits easier."

"That it will," he agreed. "That swanky joint of yours got a hot tub?"

"There's one in the room!"

He raised his eyebrows. "Better yet."

"I think I'll have something stronger than white wine tonight," she said. "How about a Rusty Nail?"

"One Rusty Nail, comin' up," said Clint as he raised a long finger to the bar tender.

"Better make it a double," said Linda as she snuggled next to Clint.

They finished their drinks listening to Hank Williams crooning, *Your Cheatin' Heart* and walked into the cold night arm in arm.

Chapter 4
Seattle, Washington

Beth

Beth typed through the Whitefish stop, slept through Spokane, and awoke as the sign for Leavenworth faded into the distance. She stowed her *Surface Pro 2,* locked her cabin door, and walked to the dining car. As the sliding door closed behind her, she noticed that Maggie was seated alone at a table next to the galley kitchen. Maggie wore the same flower-print dress with the low-slung bodice.

"Mind if I join you again?" said Beth.

"Help yourself," said Maggie as she gestured with a Bloody Mary in her hand. "Sleep well?"

"Very well. Thanks," said Beth as she settled into the seat across from Maggie. "So, you're going to Alaska. How are you getting there after you leave the train?"

"Stayin' over in Seattle one night. Found a flight to Anchorage on Alaska Airlines for a hundred and fifty bucks. Then on to Homer."

"Any chance you'd like some company?" asked Beth.

Maggie squinted at Beth in surprise. "I thought you were lookin' at bookstores."

"I'm sure there are bookstores in Anchorage, or even in Homer. With all those long, dark nights, I expect there are plenty of readers—especially when the alternative is watching bad TV or drinking cheap whiskey."

Maggie laughed and raised her glass. "If you watch television today, you have to drink." She took a long look at Beth. "Don't look to me like I'd be your kind of company—and from what Ridley has told me, I'm not that easy to live with."

Beth smiled. "I think traveling with you might be a good learning experience."

"I'll bet," smirked Maggie. "What you hopin' to learn? Maybe I could just tell you and save us the bother of travelin' together." She paused and looked at Beth skeptically. "Or are you one a those do-gooders tryin' to fix me?"

The waiter stopped at the table and directed his attention to Beth. "Coffee with cream, ma'am?"

"Thank you," said Beth. "I'm impressed you remembered—and I *did* use the cream."

The waiter smiled and glanced at Maggie. "Your table last night was memorable." Then he said, "Our breakfast special is two eggs, toast and ham."

"That would be lovely," said Beth. "Eggs over easy."

"The same," said Maggie. When the waiter left, she frowned at Beth. "Nothin' broke about me, ya know."

"Of course not," said Beth. "I'm not trying to fix anyone. I just like observing people—particularly colorful ones like you."

"Thank you…I think," said Maggie.

"And I'd be happy to share expenses," added Beth. "Maybe even cover a little more than half?"

"Hmm," considered Maggie. "I'm going to need to find a job as soon as I get to Alaska, so maybe sharin' expenses would be okay. How long would I be stuck with you if things don't work out?"

"You'd be free to tell me to leave whenever you like, but I'd appreciate fair warning. My job back home at the library is flexible, and I can easily find a sub—so my time is open-ended."

"What about your cats?" asked Maggie. "You seemed pretty attached to them. Won't they miss you?"

"Ah…my neighbor gets along with them pretty well," lied Beth. "You know cats. They can be indifferent as long as they have food, water, and a warm radiator."

The waiter set a cup of coffee on the table as he rushed by. Beth took a sip and reached for the cream. "I think my neighbor's lease is up soon. She might even like moving into my apartment for a while."

"Okay," sighed Maggie. "If we're gonna travel together, we need a few ground rules."

"I like rules," said Beth. "What did you have in mind?"

"We go fifty-fifty on expenses. I may be a little short, but I don't expect no handout."

"Fifty-fifty, then," agreed Beth. "I'm next." She pointed to her phone. "This phone and my laptop are private property."

"What?" laughed Maggie. "You got somethin' to hide—maybe some kinky porn?"

Beth opened her eyes in surprise.

"Just kiddin'," said Maggie. "Next rule of mine: No judging. And I keep my own hours—I come and go as I please."

"Agreed. No judging. I like that," said Beth. "That can work for both of us, but there's one more condition."

"What's that?" said Maggie.

"I do the cooking. You do the dishes."

"That's fine by me." said Maggie. "I hate to cook. You won't mind if I let 'em stack up between meals? I do 'em once a week at home—makes it worth my while."

"Nope." Beth shook her head. "That'll only be acceptable if I only cook once a week. I expect to start each meal with a clean kitchen."

"Picky, picky," said Maggie. She extended a freckled hand across the table and raised her eyebrows. "This makes us partners?"

Beth paused. "I guess...in a sense." Then she smiled and took Maggie's hand with a much firmer grip than when they had met over dinner.

The waiter delivered their food. Maggie lifted her nearly empty glass to Beth's coffee cup. "To our partnership."

"To our partnership."

Maggie

Am I crazy? thought Maggie as she waited for Beth on the Seattle platform. It was close to noon and the March drizzle hung over the city like a pall. *Why did I agree to this "partnership" arrangement. I'm not that poor. I had enough saved up for a few weeks while I found a job. I didn't want company. If I find a guy and want to bring him home, what am I supposed to do? Kick her out like she was a college roommate? Shit.*

Beth waved from the door of the train as she stepped out of the coach. She lugged a huge suitcase in her direction. "Sorry to keep you waiting," she said. "I needed to double check my room to make sure I didn't leave anything behind."

"It's only a six by ten room," said Maggie.

"I keep a check list when I travel." Beth pulled a list from her purse to show Maggie.

Maggie rolled her eyes and said, "Come on. Let's go. I've got a room at the *Red Roof* near the airport—only fifty-nine bucks."

"I'd rather not sleep on a cardboard bed," said Beth. "I reserved a room at the *Embassy Suites*. It's about twice that cost, but if you kick in your fifty-nine dollars, we'll both get a good night's sleep."

"All right," said Maggie. "Should I flag down a cab?"

"No need," said Beth as she popped open an umbrella. "It's only a few blocks. We can walk. After we leave our bags at the hotel, I'd like to visit a few bookstores."

"You do what you like. I'm going to visit *Pike Place Fish Market*," said Maggie. "Maybe test my skills at fish flinging."

"I'll bet you'd be good at that," laughed Beth.

Later that evening, Beth was in her flannel pajamas tapping away at her laptop when Maggie staggered into the hotel room. It was approaching one a.m.

"Who needs Alaska, eh?" boomed Maggie. "Lotsa men right here in Seattle—brawny men in beards and bibs." She flung her handbag on the floor. "They sure got my juices flowin'!"

"You smell like a fish who's spent the day swimming in a vat of beer," said Beth.

"No judging. Remember?" Maggie pulled the door shut behind her. "You shoulda come along, Beth. Might a loosened you up a bit."

"I doubt it. Where've you been all this time?"

"Like I said, started out gettin' the feel of fresh Atlantic salmon at *Pike Place*. Then got the feel of the fellas that sell 'em." She laughed heartily. "Spent a lovely afternoon at the *Blarney Stone Pub*. Never had so many free drinks."

"You catch any keepers?" chuckled Beth before she turned her attention back to her laptop.

"Not there," said Maggie as she pulled her dress over her head and dropped it on the floor next to her bag, "but on a lark, I took an Uber to *Fishermen's Terminal*."

"Why *Fishermen's Terminal*?"

"Got a tip that it's the place to find jobs in Alaska."

"How'd you do?"

"I think I may have found a job—and a keeper. What a hunk! And that sweet Aussie accent!"

"Are you always this impulsive?" called Beth as Maggie closed the door to the bathroom.

"I'll tell you all about Captain Richard tomorrow," said Maggie through the door. "I'm gonna meet him in Homer for a full interview next week."

"A full interview?" laughed Beth. "Any idea about what a 'full interview' means?"

Maggie's response was a flushing toilet.

Beth hit save and closed her laptop, then picked up Maggie's dress, folded it and set it on the dresser.

As Beth crawled into the queen bed next to the radiator, Maggie stuck her head and bare chest out the bathroom door. "You don't mind if I sleep in the nude, do ya?" she said.

Beth gasped. "Put those away, for God's sake." She pulled the covers over her head and looked the other way.

"I'll take that as a no," said Maggie as she ducked back into the bathroom. "Can you hand me a T-shirt from my suitcase?"

Chapter 5
Whitefish, Montana

Max

Max caught the first bus to Whitefish Mountain the morning after he checked into the *Hampton Inn*. He purchased his lift ticket, took the Swift Current chairlift, and skied down Lobo, then Calamity Jane. After a few warmups, he moved to the blue runs under the Ram Charger and Thunder Wolf lifts. Pleased with himself that he still had the legs, he challenged himself with the black runs of Stillwater Bowl in the afternoon.

After stowing his skis at the base of the lodge, he retired to the *Hellroaring Saloon and Eatery* where he pulled up a seat at the bar. The knotty pine walls were cluttered with Coors Light and Budweiser signs, pictures of celebrities, and the day's specials. Beer pitchers, an assortment of billed caps, and dollar bills hung from the ceiling. Max ordered a Bud Light from a bearded bartender who wore a baggy flannel shirt with suspenders that held up saggy jeans.

Halfway through Max's first beer, a young man with a well-groomed red beard sat down next to him. Max recognized him as the Headwaters lift operator. "Are you the guy who stopped the lift for me?" he said in embarrassment. "Can't believe I slipped getting onto the chair."

"Yeah. I remember you," said the young man. "Hard to forget those bright green bibs."

"Got 'em 50% off at the end-of-year sale," said Max, proudly.

"Never pass up a bargain," laughed the lift operator. "I'm Phil. This your first day?"

"Just arrived on the train last night. I'm Max."

"You here alone?"

"Not quite," said Max who emptied his beer before replying. "My wife came with me, but we decided to part company for the vacation."

"Sorry, man," said Phil. "Let me get you another beer." He waved his hand to the bartender. "Jake. One more for this gentleman." He turned back to Max. "Where you staying?"

"Got a room at the *Hampton* in town —low budget, but it'll do for now."

"How long you plan to be in town?"

Jake delivered the beer and nodded to Phil.

"Original plan was for two weeks," said Max, "but I think it'll be longer. I'm sick of my job. I'm sick of my nagging wife, and I can't bear the thought of returning to either one."

"Whoa, dude. Sounds like you're in a world of hurt."

"I guess you're right," said Max, as he thought for a moment and sipped his beer. "Things could be worse, though. I've got a few bucks stashed away, but that won't last forever. You know of anyone around here who could use a good accountant?"

Phil raised his eyebrows. "I just might," he said as he looked in Jake's direction, "I heard the *Hellroaring Saloon* just lost their bookkeeper." Phil raised his hand again to get the bartender's attention.

"Be right with you," said Jake as he set a whiskey sour on the counter for another customer, then shuffled to the other end of the bar where Max and Phil were seated. "What can I get you?"

"Jake," said Phil. "Is it true that your boss is looking for a bookkeeper?"

"That's right. As manager, I had to let the last one go. She just didn't work out."

Phil gestured to Max. "I might have found her replacement," he said. "Meet Max."

Max extended his hand to the burly bartender. "I'm Max Wharton. I'm a tax accountant, but right now I'd be happy to do some low stress bookkeeping."

"I'll do a short background check on you and talk to the boss," said Jake. "Maybe I can arrange an interview. It would only be part time."

Don't dig too deep on that background check, thought Max. "Part time would be perfect. I still want plenty of time to ski."

A young lady in a tight-fitting pink ski outfit sat down next to Phil. She took off her fur-rimmed hood and pulled her blond hair from under her collar revealing a birthmark the size of a quarter on her neck. "Hey!" she said as she gave Phil a peck on the cheek. "Am I in time for dinner?"

Phil stood from his bar stool, gave her a hug, and introduced Max. "Twila, this is Max. Max, this is Twila. He's new in town and looking for a job as a bookkeeper."

Twila sniffed once, reached across the stool, and offered Max a delicate hand. "Nice to meet you."

"Let's find a table and order food," said Phil. "I'm starving. Care to join us, Max?"

"Love to," said Max. "And thanks for the employment tip."

The three of them ordered their food at the bar and found an open table. "Have you known each other long?" asked Max.

Twila looked at Phil and said, "We met at the beginning of the ski season. I sell lift tickets and work at *The Toggery* in town. It's a clothing store." She unzipped her coat to show off her outfit. "I get twenty percent off—bought this sweater earlier in the week and the ski outfit at the beginning of the season."

"Max got a better bargain on his bibs," teased Phil. *"Fifty* percent off."

Twila gave Max an appraising look. "Won't be able to miss *you* on the hill."

"I'm ahead of the curve when it comes to fashion," laughed Max.

"And where are you staying, Max?" asked Twila.

"I'm at the *Hampton* for now," said Max.

"He and his wife have split," said Phil as he sipped his drink.

"Oh. Sorry to hear that," said Twila.

"That's okay," said Max. "I think it's temporary…but who knows?"

"Are you looking for a more permanent place to live?" asked Twila. "I don't think the *Hampton* rents by the month."

Max chuckled. "No. It fits my budget for now, but I'll need to find another place soon—particularly if I land a job here at the restaurant."

"We're staying in a small cabin within walking distance of town," said Phil. "It's one of several cabins that were once a small resort. A buddy of mine who was another chairlift operator just moved out. The landlord is looking for new renter."

"That would be great," said Max. "Do you know what the rent will be?"

"It's pretty cheap—especially compared to hotel prices. Just remember to turn down the heat during the day."

The bartender delivered Angus burgers to Phil and Max and a chicken Caesar salad to Twila.

Phil picked up his burger and looked at Max before taking a bite. "What do you think, Max? Are you interested?"

"Sounds perfect," said Max. "I'll check out of the *Hampton* as soon as you hear from your landlord."

Twila swallowed a bite of salad and said, "I'm off tomorrow. How about you, Phil? I'd like to ski the bowls."

"Sorry," said Phil. "Gotta' work all day."

"I don't like to ski back there alone," said Twila. "How 'bout you, Max? Are you available?"

Max turned to Phil with a questioning look. Phil nodded in Twila's direction. "Go for it, Max. Twila's right. No one should ski alone in the back bowls."

"Okay, Twila. Meet you at the bottom of lift six around nine?"

"Let's make it ten."

"Right. See you at ten."

"If you need anything else," said Phil, "just let me know. I've got lots of connections."

As Max was leaving the bar, he noticed that Jake had taken his place at the table. Jake glanced over his shoulder at Max before returning to their huddled conversation.

Hmm, thought Max. *They all seem to know each other pretty well.*

Max caught the bus into town that would take him within a couple of blocks of the *Hampton Inn*. As he settled into a seat at the rear of the bus, he thought about his son, Clyde. *I hope he's not trashing the house.* Max closed his eyes and leaned against the window. *When he was little, we used to take him skiing all the time. I was the one who taught him to ski. Linda always found an excuse to ski by herself. Clyde and I got along pretty well until his teens. Those were rough years.*

When Clyde turned twenty-one, he wanted to come along again—and have me pay, of course. Caused another row with Linda. I told her that if Clyde's goal in life was to become a ski bum, he needed to start paying his own way. Max felt the bus come to a stop. As he stepped off the bus, he continued his musing. *He's a handsome kid—tall, auburn hair, straight teeth, lanky build, has lots of girlfriends, but no commitment—to anything. Doesn't look much like me, but I suppose we're alike in a lot of ways. I wanted the same thing he did when I was his age.*

Max felt his heartrate pick up. *Four years of college, and nothing to show for it. Jesus H. Christ. Get a job, Clyde!* He jerked hard on the door to the *Hampton.*

Chapter 6
Homer, Alaska

Beth

After a flight to Anchorage and a hopper to Homer, Beth and Maggie secured an off-season rate at *Jenny Way Cottage*. Maggie liked it because it was near the *Elks Lodge* and *AJ's Old Tavern*. Beth liked it because it was only a twenty-minute walk to the *Homer Public Library*. It was a tiny cabin with blue siding and a metal roof. A half-dozen wooden steps on its north side led to the front door, which opened into a kitchen and living room on the right and a bedroom crammed with two single beds on the left.

Beth and Maggie sat at a small wooden table and sipped their morning coffee.

"Wow! This tastes better than what you've been servin' the last week," exclaimed Maggie.

"You noticed! I ordered a new coffee maker and espresso machine—a *De' Longhi COM530M*," said Beth proudly. "It arrived yesterday. I couldn't take another cup from that rusted out *Mr. Coffee*."

"The cream in the frig will probably go sour now," laughed Maggie.

They gazed south through the picture window, which overlooked the Kachemak Bay and the Chugach Mountains.

"Did you get the job with Captain Richard?" asked Beth.

"You bet I did," said Maggie. "I'm gonna be a deckhand on his boat—the *Red Tempest*. He says it's a seiner—for salmon fishin', but it don't leave port 'til mid-May when the season opens."

"It's the end of March now. What are you going to do until then?"

"Dick says there's plenty of maintenance that I can help with—mending nets, painting, engine maintenance, and stocking the boat with supplies."

"Do you know anything about Alaskan fishing?" said Beth. "I expect the captain would prefer someone with experience."

Maggie tipped a shot of Jim Beam into her coffee cup and smiled. "I gave the captain an interview that he'll never forget." She took a sip and licked her lips. "By the time I walked off the dock, he gave me the job—told me enthusiasm and stamina are more important than experience."

Beth shook her head and smiled. "Sounds like you were very persuasive. Did you ask him if you lived up to the name of his boat."

Maggie laughed. "After my performance, if the boat *hadn't* been named the *Red Tempest*, he probably would have re-named it in my honor."

"I've got to meet this captain of yours," said Beth. "Didn't you call him 'a hunk?'"

"He's a hunk all right," said Maggie. "I'm sure he's not your type, but we can meet at *AJ's Tavern* after work sometime soon."

"I'd like that," said Beth. *Not my type*, she thought, *but Captain Dick sounds like he could be the hero I'm looking for in my book. I wonder if he's for real.*

Beth refilled her cup. "I got a job, too, but my interview didn't require as much athleticism as yours did."

"Who hired you?" said Maggie. "Is Homer in need of a librarian?"

"Matter of fact, it is," said Beth. "I've got a part-time job with the *Homer Public Library*."

"Sounds very dull. I thought you came here for adventure."

"I did," said Beth, "but some of us can have adventures in our mind that are just as satisfying as having them in person."

"That's a little hard to believe—that it can be *just* as satisfying," said Maggie, "but like you, I like a good book once in a while." She reached for her copy of *Romance of Lady Candue*. Just about finished with this one and looking forward to the next book in the series."

"Interesting that you mentioned Lady Candue," said Beth. "I noticed that the library has invited Lance Freeport to give a reading from his latest novel sometime next month. You could have your books autographed."

"That's amazing!" said Maggie. "How did they ever get someone like him to come to this hole-in-the-wall?"

"Maybe he needed some in-person adventure to spice up his writing."

Chapter 7
Whitefish, Montana

Linda

Linda woke to the sound of Clint snoring. He sprawled next to her in the king-sized bed in her suite at the Whitefish Lake Lodge. He smelled of aftershave, cigars, and sex. She stepped onto the floor and slipped on a white terrycloth robe—compliments of the lodge. She walked to the window. The frozen lake glittered in the morning sunshine. In the distance, the lifts below the runs on the western edge of Whitefish Mountain were coming to life.

She padded over to the kitchenette and plugged in the coffee maker. Clint woke to the sound and smell of fresh-brewed coffee and called from the bedroom, "You up already? I thought you'd sleep in after that romp we had last night."

"I did sleep in, you wild man," said Linda. She walked into the bedroom, handed him a mug, and sat down on the bed next to him. "It's nearly ten."

"My, my, so it is," said Clint as he stole a glance at the clock and then at Linda's parted robe.

"Didn't you get your fill last night?" laughed Linda as she pulled the robe over her crossed legs. "I thought that more than once was only for teenagers."

"Nah," chuckled Clint. He set his cup on the end table and reached for her waist. "I was just getting warmed up."

Linda leaned over and gave him a kiss as his hand slipped inside her robe. She pushed his hand away and said, "Let's save it for tonight. I came here to ski, too."

"Oh, alright. If you insist," said Clint. "How about some breakfast and we'll catch the afternoon runs?"

"I think they quit serving breakfast at ten thirty, so we better hurry."

She turned away and dropped her robe on the floor, knowing he'd be watching. She slowly stepped into a pair of bright red panties.

"Do I look as good here as I did in the video you took last night?"

Clint laughed. "Let's watch it together this evening. You can be the judge…but that's a hell of a body you got there, Linda."

She turned her face to him with a coy expression. "Glad to hear you appreciate it. I work at it." She thought for a moment and said, "You know? I could get used to living here."

"I'll bet they'd like to have a woman like you over at the fitness center," said Clint as he climbed out of bed and began to dress.

Another compliment. Max never seems to notice all I do to keep my body in shape—and for what?

"You think they have an opening over there?" she said as she pulled a sports bra over her head. "I've been thinking of staying in Whitefish longer, so I could use a part-time job." She cupped her hands under her breasts and fit them into the bra.

"Let me make some calls," said Clint as he pulled jeans over his long, pale legs. "I know some people in town that might be able to help you out." He shrugged into his western-style shirt and continued. "If you stuck around, where would you stay? I doubt you can afford to stay in this place very long."

"I just received a windfall from my parents' estate," she said, "but I wouldn't want to spend it all on a fancy hotel." She stepped into a pair of tights and pulled a turtleneck over her head. "I've got this room reserved for the next couple of weeks, but after that I'd need to find something else that's cheaper. Of course, if I made a quick trip to a local casino, I could afford to extend our stay here."

"Save your winnings," said Clint, "I've got a cabin that I rent for the season up in the woods not far from town. There's no hot tub, but I've got a shower with plenty of hot water—and a bed that rocks. How about stayin' there?"

"Don't you have other guests? I wouldn't want to impose."

"Nothing regular," he laughed. "After last night, there's no competition."

Linda pulled on a pair of Nike sneakers and looked Clint in the eye. "About that video—just for us. Right? No one else sees them?"

"Just for us," repeated Clint, "but I'll bet you'll love it."

Linda smiled. "Let's have breakfast."

Chapter 8
Homer, Alaska

Beth

Beth stared into the bay through their picture window. "Look at this fog," she said to Maggie. "It's so thick, I can't see the Chugach Mountains."

"It's a lot like the fog that rolls across Lake Superior," said Maggie as she pulled up a chair.

Beth set two plates heaped with scrambled eggs and French toast on the table.

Maggie sawed off a piece of French toast and dipped it in a pool of syrup. "You sure had me fooled last night at the library." She pointed the fork at Beth in a menacing gesture and laughed. "You should be ashamed of yourself for not telling me before now. When you told me Lance Freeport would be in town, I never dreamed it was you."

Beth smiled and sat down next to her. "In the writing world we call that suspense."

"Huh," said Maggie as she scooped up a fork full of eggs. "You shouldn't keep a friend in suspense like that."

"Sorry," said Beth. "I'll try to be more forthright in the future."

"What else you been hidin' from me?" said Maggie. "How about tellin' me how ya came to be a writer? It's time to fess up and empty the skeletons from your closet."

"There are no skeletons," said Beth as she took a sip of coffee. "It's kind of a dull story. Are you sure you're interested?"

"Got nothin' better to do this mornin'. Dick said there's no need to come in 'til noon today. Shoot."

"I was bored with school," said Beth. "I used to read romance novels at my desk while my teachers droned on about cell biology, the Civil War, or the Pythagorean Theorem. I could figure out what I needed to know by reading the textbooks before the tests. I was also an only child, so I had plenty of time to myself at home. I read every Nora Roberts book. Did you know they call her 'The Queen of the Romance Novel?'"

"Nope," said Maggie, "but I read a couple a' hers too. They're real good. I can see why they call her that."

"As a kid, I also loved to write. I kept a diary from the time I was in third grade." Beth laughed. "I still have them—or my parents do—if they haven't thrown them out."

"You're famous now," said Maggie. "They're probably pretty valuable, don't you think?"

"If you're a blackmailer, I suppose they are," chuckled Beth. She nibbled at her eggs. "I never had much luck with boys. I knew I wasn't that cute or particularly beautiful, but boys still kept asking me out."

She cradled her coffee cup in her hand and gazed at the fog. "At our last class reunion, I heard there was a bet going around— about which boy could cop a feel of my boob...I suppose I was kind of intimidating because I was at the top of my class. Those boys were handsome, but they were so arrogant—they dropped me as soon as I slapped their hands."

Maggie laughed and pointed a finger at Beth's chest. "Wouldn't take much to get a hand on those little lemons. You musta been a vicious little fox." She cupped her hands under her own breasts. "Now these beauties...They were worth the chase."

"So, you enjoyed getting groped by those horny high school boys?"

"Naw. I just teased 'em. They knew their limits. I'd a slugged 'em if they got too fresh."

"I'm embarrassed to admit it," said Beth, "but I enjoyed the attention. I can only imagine how those boys took out their frustrations when they got home, but I could always retreat to my diary. I'd include all the details—what cologne they wore, the questions they asked to make me think they were as smart as I was, their sweaty hands, the buttered popcorn stains on their jeans—but I'd always write a better ending than the ones I experienced."

"That ain't nuthin' to be embarrassed about," said Maggie. "We had to be on guard. It kept us outa the maternity wards 'til we were ready—not that either of us will ever be ready for that."

"Guess you're right. In any case, my parents thought I should use my smarts and writing skills to become a journalist."

"I took their advice and enrolled at University of Minnesota Hubbard School of Journalism. I hoped to become as famous as Judy Woodruff at PBS or Bob Woodward at the Washington Post. You know—sleuthing out injustice, exposing graft, running selfish politicians out of office. I had high hopes for college, but I didn't realize how introverted I was. We had to interview people—get in their face, you know? We had to speak in front of crowds. I was terrified of that."

"You must have gotten over it," said Maggie. "You looked pretty comfortable at your library talk."

"I've gotten better, but it reminds me of a Jerry Seinfeld bit where he said, 'Studies have shown that people's number one fear is public speaking. Number two is death…So if you go to a funeral, you're better off being in the casket than giving the eulogy.'"

"Ha!" said Maggie. "The funerals I've been to are filled with lies about whoever's in the coffin. Nobody would ask me to speak. They'd worry I'd be too honest."

"That's the problem with journalism, too," said Beth. "I loved to write, but it was more fun for me to write fiction. I turned in essays and research papers, and all I got from my professors was ridicule: Write something serious, Beth. Your work is so superficial. This isn't literature or journalism. This is crap."

"At the beginning of my senior year," she continued, "I published my first novel based on my diary entries. It's the one you were reading on the train: *The Romance of Lady Candue*— and it became a best seller!"

"Your first try, and it was a best seller?"

"I decided I didn't need any more college, so I dropped out. My parents didn't think much of my decision, and as I look back, they probably were right. Turns out, I'm trapped in my success. My agent keeps demanding another book. I keep cranking it out, and my readers keep buying them. My last one was called *Lady Candue Wrestles with Success*. I don't know how to get off the hamster wheel."

Chapter 9
Whitefish, Montana

Max

Six inches of fresh powder had fallen overnight, and the snowcats were packing the runs when Max arrived at the bottom of lift six. He stood to the side of the lift line watching snowboarders in baggy pants and crowds of teenagers on spring break waiting to be swept up the mountain. A few minutes after ten, Twila skidded to a stop next to him.

"Hey, Max. You ready to take on the bowls?"

"Absolutely," said Max as he sucked in his belly and gazed briefly at Twila's perfect contours. "Can't beat a new snowfall for bowl skiing." He dropped his skies on the ground and stepped into the bindings. "Let's go get 'em."

Twila bent over and tightened her boots with a trembling hand.

"Can I help you with that?" asked Max.

"No. I can get it. Thanks."

The couple settled into the chairlift and Max pulled down the safety bar. "Can you tell me about the bookkeeping job at the *Hellroaring Saloon and Eatery*?" he asked. "Is that legit?"

"Yeah. I know Jake, the bartender. He's a good guy, but he didn't get along with the old bookkeeper. I think she was kind of pushy." Twila cocked her head. "You know men. They don't like to be told what to do—particularly by a woman."

"My wife could vouch for that," said Max.

"Sorry to hear you and your wife are having problems."

"Thanks. I shouldn't have said anything at dinner last night. It's not your problem."

"Well, if there's anything I can do, just let me know."

"A recommendation for the accounting job might be helpful," said Max.

"I don't know much about your professional skills, but I know Jake pretty well. I'd be happy to put in a word on your behalf."

Max gave Twila a short summary of his background: CPA from *Carlson School of Business*, tax expert with *Henderson Accounting*, and a major client that had been happy with his work. "But I'm ready for a change," he concluded. "I need something without so much stress."

Twila wiped her nose with a tissue. "Sorry. The cold gives me a runny nose."

The lift approached the unloading area and Twila lifted the safety bar. "With your background," she said, "you'd be a shoo-in for the job."

"Thanks. I'll talk to Jake this afternoon."

Max struggled to keep up with Twila as she led him down one run of deep powder after another, but he was finding his rhythm by noon. After lunch at the *Shedhorn Grill*, they were content to finish the day on groomed blue runs.

As they skied to the chalet after their last run, Max said, "Thanks for guiding me around the mountain today. You free again tomorrow?"

"I'm working at *The Toggery* tomorrow morning, but I'm free in the evening. How about dinner and a drink at the *Hellroaring Saloon*?"

"Won't Phil be concerned if he finds out that we're having dinner together?"

"Ah, you worry too much," said Twila. "He's got girlfriends lined up all over the mountain."

"Well, how about a late lunch?" suggested Max. "That might be safer."

Chapter 10
Homer, Alaska

Maggie

It was the last of April and Maggie was slowly adjusting to sixteen hours of sunlight. She had spent most of her days—and nights—with Cap'n Dick, the affectionate name she had assigned him. She found the rigors of fresh air and boat maintenance exhilarating—and she found the rigorous exercise on the captain's king bed even more so. He did not mind her preference for sleeping in the nude, and she did not mind the nights away from the cramped single bed at *Jenny Way Cottage.*

Maggie had become a regular at *AJ's OldTown Steakhouse and Tavern.* Its metal-roof awning sprawled across the front of the restaurant, sheltering the door and the wooden benches that rested on either side. The place specialized in chalkboard advertising with "Open at 5," scrawled on the board next to the door and "Daily Specials" posted on the blackboard next to the well-stocked bar. Wood-grain paneling surrounded a spacious dining room. Black swivel stools lined the bar. Chairs with red vinyl seats sat next to tables decorated with blue tablecloths.

A lean, fifty-something man wearing a white T-shirt, a white cowboy hat, and a white goatee occupied a small stage. He strummed a white guitar singing Johnny Cash favorites.

Maggie and Cap'n Dick had secured a permanent dinner reservation in a corner booth. Cap'n Dick wore his brown, shoulder-length hair swept back over his forehead. A recent scar over his left eye had contracted as it healed. It lifted his eyebrow and made him appear persistently skeptical. A three-day stubble masked his ruddy complexion and complemented his angular features.

Maggie had been sipping a Jim Beam and Dick nursed a Johnnie Walker Scotch on the rocks when Beth walked into the bar and looked around.

"Over here," shouted Maggie as she gestured to the empty seat at the booth. "Meet my good friend, Captain Richard Fleshman—Captn' Dick. Dick, I'd like you to meet Lance Freeport, my favorite author."

Beth blushed as she offered her hand to Dick. "I've heard a lot about you from Maggie. I'm Beth Lancer. Lance Freeport is my pen name."

"G'day," said Dick as he rose, took her hand, and kissed it lightly. "How ya going?"

"Aren't you a charmer," said Beth as they took their seats. Maggie slid next to Dick and Beth sat across from them.

"I heard your talk at the library last week was right crikey," said Dick. "The wives of every man on the dock must have attended your book signing."

"Of course, I was there too," said Maggie. She took a drink of her Beam and wagged an accusing finger at Beth. "Now I know why you write using a pen name."

Beth smiled and nodded.

Maggie explained to Dick, "I was embarrassed to carry my entire *Lady Candue* collection to the library that night, only to find out I could have had 'em all signed at home."

Beth laughed. "Lucky you had your own collection. I sold out that night."

"Now I know why your luggage was so heavy," said Maggie. "You really surprised your audience at the library—all those women waitin' for a handsome man to take the podium."

"I suppose they were disappointed to find that Lance Freeport was not who they had expected," said Beth. She glanced at Dick. "Isn't that so often the case?"

Dick's left eye jumped imperceptibly, but he quickly laughed and turned the gesture into a wink. "That's true, mate," he said. "Happens whenever I try to hire a crew—damn hard to find good help these days."

"It sounds like you may have found a good deckhand in Maggie, though," said Beth. "I understand she'll be joining your jolly band of pirates on this year's expedition."

Captain Dick smiled broadly and took Maggie's hand. "Yeah. She's the True Blue—a heaps good addition to the crew."

"How many people does it take to crew your boat?" asked Beth.

"The *Red Tempest* is a fifty-eight-foot seiner. We have a total of five crew on the boat: two deckhands, an engineer, a skiff man, and a captain. I'm the captain. I find the fish and fight for a spot to lower the net."

Dick waved a hand to the bay. "It's a dog-eat-dog world out there," he sighed. "Sometimes ya gotta out-maneuver other boats to get the prime fishing spots."

Dick downed the remainder of his drink and waved to the waitress. "The skiff man," he continued, "tows the lead end of the seine toward a school of fish, circles the school, and returns to the boat."

"Tell me about the skiff." said Beth. "I used to drive a good-sized boat on Lake Superior. My parents had a cabin on the Wisconsin shore. My dad loved to fish for lake trout. He'd troll while I took the wheel, but that was years ago."

"The skiff's a small motorboat that is towed behind the seiner for most of the voyage," said Dick with a patient voice. "The deep-water net is a seine that's connected to a purse line. It acts as a drawstring to enclose the catch."

"Fascinating," said Beth. "What does the rest of the crew do?"

"Two mates are the deckhands. They stack and prepare the net for each set, or catch, and dump the fish into the hold when the net is ready to be emptied. The engineer maintains the engines, pumps, and runs the winches and the boom—the long arm that hauls in the net when it's full of fish."

A waitress wearing a pale complexion and a dark knit sweater arrived to take their orders: king crab and asparagus for Beth, ribeye for Maggie, and a filet for Cap'n Dick. Maggie and Dick ordered another round of drinks and Beth ordered coffee.

"Sounds exciting, don't you think?" said Maggie, as she delivered a charming smile to Cap'n Dick.

"Very," said Beth. "How long are you out at sea once you leave the dock?"

"Our early season run will be 'bout six weeks," said Dick. "If we're lucky, we'll be back in time for the Fourth of July."

"My, that's a long time to be away from dry land," said Beth. "What do you do with the fish you catch if you don't return to port?"

"Big vessels called tenders collect the fish from the smaller boats like ours. We ice the fish in a refrigerated hold until we off-load them to the big boats. There are some, even bigger ships called factory trawlers that process and package the fish on board."

"Mid-May is only two weeks away," observed Beth. "Do you have a full crew?"

"My engineer is returning this season. but I had some bloody bad luck the end of last season," he said sadly. "These Eskimos are a superstitious bunch and don't wanna sign on with me this year."

"What happened?" asked Beth.

The waitress delivered their drinks and Dick swallowed half his glass before she left the table. "Had a deckhand named Siku. I told the flamin' galah we had a frayed cable on the boom, and it was his job to replace it. The bludger didn't follow my orders." He shook his head in dismay. "Bloody hell…He paid dearly for that mistake."

Dick gulped the remainder of his drink before he continued. "It was the last run of the season, and we were haulin' in the biggest catch we had all year. Just as the boom swung over the starboard gunwale, the cable snapped." Dick squinted at the table. "Poor bugger didn't see it coming. The end of the cable nicked the chin of another one of my Eskimos. He's doin' fine, but the cable smacked Siku on the side of his face—hard." Dick's voice rose with emotion. "Next thing I know, he's thrashing around in the water surrounded by a pool of blood that was gettin' bigger every second. I was in the wheelhouse and hollered at Bert—he's my engineer—told him to drop the bloody net full of fish into the ocean. 'Forget the fish,' I shouted. 'We gotta man overboard, for God's sake.'"

Dick's eyes widened as he related the frightful story. "I don't know if Bert heard me, but by the time I got to the deck to help pull Siku out of the water, it was too late. I had to grab his slicker with a gaff hook to get him onto the boat. I tried to revive him, but we were too late. Nothin' I could do."

No one spoke for several minutes until Beth broke the silence. "Did Siku have a family?"

"A wife and one kid," said Dick. "I filed an insurance claim, and the family got a nice settlement." He shrugged his shoulders. "The family was probably better off getting' the settlement than if Siku had stayed workin'. Those Eskimos piss away most of their pay on frothies before their families see a dime."

"I heard they'd rather be called Inuit than Eskimo." Said Beth.

"Same thing," said Dick.

"Is Bert Inuit?"

"Naw. He's a chubby little dag that couldn't pull a perch out of the water, but he can run a crane like a pro—and he knows engines."

"So, do the Inuits believe you're bad luck?" pressed Beth.

"I guess that's what most of 'em think," replied Dick, "but last week I persuaded Hanta—that's my Eskimo who got cut up a little—to sign on again as a deckhand. With Maggie here who agreed to be my second deckhand, all I need now is a skiff man. I was counting on last year's returning, but I just got a letter from her sayin' she's not coming back." His jaws clenched. "If that damn sheila knew she wasn't coming back, least she could have done is let me know before now."

The pale waitress delivered their food and refilled Beth's coffee cup. "Anything else?" she said.

Dick gestured to the empty glasses in front of him and Maggie. "Fill 'em up, mate."

Beth picked at her king crab while Maggie and Dick sliced into their beef.

Maggie swallowed a piece of steak and took a sip of water. "Beth, any chance you'd like to join the crew?" She turned to Dick and said, "She already told you she knows how to drive a motorboat…and she's a hell of a good cook. What do you think?"

Dick chewed on his filet before replying, "I don't know, Mag. She doesn't look like she has the stamina for going to sea. She's as puny as a pink salmon."

Beth smiled. "I didn't say I'd take the job, even if you offered it to me."

Maggie gave Beth a pleading stare. "Come on, Beth. What do you say?" She returned to look at Dick. "She's tougher than she looks—and she's a fast learner."

"What are the sleeping arrangements on the boat?" asked Beth.

"I have a private berth in the bow," said Dick. "Everyone else shares a room just behind it with four bunks—two on each side of a narrow aisle. There's a shower like you'd find in a camper, and each person gets a private locker. The galley's behind the sleeping quarters as you enter the cabin from the stern."

Beth finished her meal. Maggie had not touched her last drink but continued to give Beth encouraging glances.

Beth set her fork on her plate. "Well," she said, "the *Jenny Way Cottage* is booked at the end of the month, so I'll need someplace else to stay." Then she looked at Dick. "I have a feeling I ought to come along."

"Crikey!" said Dick. "You're hired as ship's cook and skiff man. Come to the docks tomorrow, and we'll begin your training."

Beth

The weather was clear and calm as Beth and Maggie stepped on board the *Red Tempest* to learn the skills of purse seining. The other two crew members were already on deck.

"This is Hanta," said Captain Dick. "He's the one who got nicked in the face." He looked closely at Hanta's chin. "Looks like you're healin' up pretty well, my boy."

Hanta nodded without smiling.

Beth extended her hand. "Hello Hanta. I'm Beth Lancer."

Hanta was a middle-aged Inuit. He had no facial hair, which made him look younger than he was. His sullen expression was marked with piercing brown eyes and wispy black hair that fell to one side of his forehead. Beth tried not to stare at the deep scar on the cleft of his chin. *Should have had stitches*, she thought.

"Hanta's been helping me learn the ropes," said Maggie. She gave him an affectionate tap on his shoulder. "Don't look so serious. Beth's a much faster learner than I am. This is gonna be fun."

"That's Bert," said Dick pointing to a stocky man in a red plaid shirt who was sitting in the wheelhouse above the deck. "He's the ship's engineer—my other returning crew mate."

Bert waved in greeting to the new crew members through his open window. As Dick looked away, Bert lifted his middle finger in a mock salute and then used it to push his glasses to his face.

Dick climbed the ladder to join Bert in the wheelhouse and started the engine. "Shove off, Hanta!" cried Dick. "We'll run out to the bay and practice setting the net. Then we'll see if the little lass can really run a skiff."

"Aye, Skipper," said Hanta with no enthusiasm. He stepped onto the dock, removed the lines from the cleats, and jumped back on the boat as Dick put it in gear and headed the *Red Tempest* into the bay.

The skiff, an oval-shaped, eighteen-foot boat trailed behind the stern. Maggie pointed to the skiff and said, "You'll be the skipper of that boat."

"It reminds me of a floating bathtub," said Beth.

Hanta overheard Beth's comment and offered a word of explanation. "You'll find it's perfect for the job."

While they cruised out of the harbor, Maggie pointed out what she had learned about seining. "That cable holds the skiff to the stern of the seiner while we're heading out to sea. It'll be attached to the lead end of the net when the skiff is released into the water during a set. The purse line is connected to the lower, weighted side of the net and runs through a series of grommets called purse rings—kind of like an upside-down flexible curtain rod." She pointed to a boom above their heads. "Bert operates the hydraulic winch. That pulley reels in the net when it's full of fish."

Hanta listened intently to Maggie's explanation and nodded his approval.

"See that cable with all those yellow floats attached to it?" said Maggie. "That's the cork line and it keeps the top of the net floating on the surface while you circle the fish."

"That all makes sense," said Beth.

The *Red Tempest* slowed to an idle. "We're here," shouted Captain Dick. "Let's get on with it."

"Climb aboard the skiff," said Hanta to Beth. He assisted her as she clambered over the bow. "Use the on-board radio and headset to communicate with Bert. He'll give you instructions from the wheelhouse."

Beth took a seat at the console, then looked up at Bert, who gave her a friendly wave. "Start her up," shouted Hanta.

Beth turned the key. The six-cylinder inboard coughed. She tried again and the engine sputtered to life. She raised a thumbs up and Bert let the skiff slip into the water by reversing the winch holding the skiff to the ship with the tow cable. When there was adequate slack in the cable, Hanta released the tow line from the skiff and attached it to the purse line. Beth backed the skiff from the seiner, turned it in the opposite direction, and pulled the net off the stern to begin the set.

Bert called Beth on the radio. "Drive the skiff in a wide arc. The captain will drive the *Tempest* in an arc the opposite direction." The cork line with its string of yellow buoys, played out over the stern of the trawler while the purse line and the weighted net fell over the stern next to it.

"Well done," said Bert, as the last of the cork line went over the side and the tow cable tightened against the net. "You and the skipper will complete the circle to trap our catch in the seine."

Fifteen minutes later, Bert called into the microphone, "Perfect, Beth. Now pull up next to us on our starboard side."

Beth maneuvered the skiff as directed. Maggie reached over the gunwale, grabbed the clip end of the tow line from the skiff, walked across the deck, and attached it to the far side of the seiner. Hanta unhooked the cork line from the skiff and clipped it to a cleat on the near side of the seiner. Maggie returned to separate the purse line from the cork line and attached it to the pursing winch.

"Good job, Beth," said Bert over the radio. "Now drive the skiff slowly away from the port side of the boat. When your tow line is taught, you will be pulling against the side of the seiner. You'll be pulling in the opposite direction of the net and will keep us from listing too far while the seine is being drawn over the pully on the boom that hangs over the starboard gunwale."

Beth followed Bert's directions and tightened the tow line with the skiff.

"Good," confirmed Bert again. "The skiff is in position so we can close the net and collect the fish. Rev your engine, Beth. I'm going to begin retrieving the purse line with the winch. That closes up the bottom of the net and turns it into a purse— hopefully full of King salmon."

As Bert wound in the purse line, Maggie coiled the slack rope neatly on the deck so it wouldn't tangle for the next set. When the end of the purse line reached the winch, Hanta ran a ring bar through the purse rings that had been drawn up to the side of the ship.

"All right," said Bert. "We're pursed up. Now we're ready to haul in the cork line and net so that we can snare the fish." He swiveled the boom to the edge of the starboard deck and pulled the lever for the hydraulic winch.

While Bert drew the net through the power block, Hanta and Maggie worked together on the stern deck. Hanta collected the cork line with the top of the net and laid it on a pile while Maggie did the same with the lead line—the weighted line on the bottom of the net.

The seine hung beneath the boom on the starboard side of the boat like a limp sack of potatoes. "All that's left is to pull the catch over the gunwale and onto the deck," said Bert to Beth. "I'll finish drawing in the lines. Then you can return the skiff to the stern of the trawler."

Bert lifted the purse seine onto the deck. This was a training set and it only contained bits of seaweed, a large assortment of jellyfish, and a few out-of-season salmon. Maggie and Hanta emptied the contents onto the deck and then swept the lot through the scuppers and back into the ocean.

"Crikey! That's good as gold," shouted Captain Dick. He had been keeping the ship in position and had left the training to Bert and Hanta. "Let's run through a few more sets, so it becomes second nature. Weather permitting, we'll go out three times a week until the season opens."

Bert pushed his glasses over his pug nose again and smiled into his microphone. "Beth, you even impressed Captain Dick," he said. "Let's do it again. Show him it's not a fluke."

Beth waited for Hanta and Maggie to re-attach the cork line and purse line to the skiff. She pulled away from the *Red Tempest* and said, "Nothing to it."

Chapter 11
Whitefish, Montana

Max

A small enclave of log cabins was nestled into the side of the mountain west of Whitefish. Fourteen cabins—seven on each side of an old logging road—made up the small neighborhood. Max moved into the last cabin on a dead end, the one nearest the empty cul de sac. All the cabins appeared to share the same floorplan with two steps to a small, covered deck facing the road. Each cabin had two windows—one next to the door and the other looked out the back into the pine forest. The interior was like an efficiency apartment. A small bathroom with a shower was to the left of the door. Beyond that was a tiny kitchenette with a sink and hotplate. A table with two chairs sat to the right of the door, and a queen bed with a heavy, plaid quilt occupied the far corner.

Most of his neighbors were seasonal workers and students with temporary visas. They spoke an eclectic variety of accents— Eastern European, Spanish, Scandinavian, and one German. Phil and Twila occupied the first cabin on Max's side of the street. Max had not seen the person who occupied the middle cabin down the street and across from his, but the young man with the German accent described him as a "wanabe cowboy"—tall and bow-legged. He smoked cigars and spoke with a western twang.

Max soon learned why the road had assumed a variety of local nicknames: *Lover's Lane* to the high school boys, *Lecherous Lane* to the girls, and *Lawless Lane* to the local police. Friday night the cul de sac turned into a parking lot filled with steamy pickup windows and old Chevys, the occupants of which were happily exchanging bodily fluids or baggies of weed. The vehicles dispersed only after red lights flashed against his bedroom wall.

Max had settled into his new lodging and accepted the job as bookkeeper for the *Hellroaring Saloon*. He established a new and very comfortable routine. Much to his surprise, Twila had taken a liking to him. He managed to arrange a discreet mid-day rendezvous with her several times a week. He lent her a few bucks now and then, knowing that he wouldn't get repaid. *But what the hell. She's worth it.*

Chapter 12
Homer, Alaska

Maggie

Maggie and Beth arrived at the dock promptly at six a.m. on May 15, the fishing opener for King salmon. The *Red Tempest* bobbed peacefully in the wake of another seiner that passed the pier and made its way out to sea. The net and yellow buoys filled the deck of the *Tempest*. The sound of banging crates came from within the cabin.

Maggie stepped onto the deck while Beth waited on the dock. Each woman carried a duffel bag of personal effects and a bundle of newly purchased rain gear: bright orange Brigg jackets, matching Hercules bib pants, Atlas PVC gloves, and shiny XTRATUF neoprene boots. In anticipation of the brisk ocean air, they packed Cuddl Duds, wool sweaters, and matching stocking caps.

Beth followed Maggie onto the deck and whispered, "I squeezed my Surface Pro 2 computer into my bag. Maybe I'll have some free time to write."

"Can you keep it dry?" said Maggie. "It might have been safer to bring along a ballpoint and a couple of legal pads."

Beth assured her, "It's sealed in plastic. It'll be fine."

Maggie smiled at her friend. "I noticed that you also smuggled your prized coffee maker on board on our last training run."

"Yeah. You know how much I need a good cup of coffee. The coffee maker's under the sink. I squeezed it between two bags of rice."

Captain Dick emerged from the cabin and squinted into the bright sunlight.

"Reporting for duty as directed," shouted Maggie playfully.

Dick had cut his shoulder-length hair and replaced it with a crewcut. He covered it immediately with a white captain's hat. He looked at his watch. "You're late," he said. "Time's a'wasting."

"I thought we were right on time," said Maggie. "You told us to be here at six."

"I said we *depart* at six," said Dick irritably. "Any crew member worth his rations knows enough to be on deck at least an hour ahead of time."

"Come on, Dick," said Maggie as she lifted her bags. "Lighten up. Okay if we stow our gear?"

Dick frowned and growled, "Rattle your dags!" Then he added, "Once you step on board my boat, you address me as 'Captain.' Understood?" The scar over his left eye turned a shade of red.

"What's gotten into you?" said Maggie, "and what's with the severe crewcut?"

"Ship discipline. May as well get used to it," said Dick in a clipped cadence. It's for your own safety. And long hair? It's a bloody mess at sea. Short hair is easier to keep clean. Showers only allowed twice a week, so keep yours tied back."

The captain turned to Beth who was also holding her duffle bag. "G'day, little lass. I'll take my brekky in the wheelhouse. The galley's right in there," he said pointing to the door to the cabin.

"I know where the galley is," she replied icily. "I'll call you captain, but you'll call me Beth."

"Ooh, touchy," drawled Dick. He looked away and said over his shoulder, "I take my coffee black—gave up tea when I left Australia." He ducked through the cabin door, then his head reappeared. "Everyone meets on deck at 0800."

Beth offered a mock salute as Dick retreated. She asked Maggie, "What's up with him?"

Maggie shrugged. "He's never been like this. I'll bet he's just nervous about finding enough fish. It'll be fine. I'll stow your gear while you make breakfast."

Beth

Beth followed Maggie into the galley, pulled her deluxe coffee maker from its hiding place, found the breakfast supplies, and within a half hour delivered steaming mugs of coffee and plates of scrambled eggs and pancakes to the crew.

Her first delivery was to the wheelhouse where Captain Dick was seated at a console surrounded by flickering screens and dials: LORAN Navigation equipment, fish-finders, radar, GPS, compass, and a satellite Vessel Monitoring System. "Impressive setup," she said as she handed Dick a steaming mug. "Hard to get lost out here with all of that equipment, huh?"

Dick took a sip of coffee. "Bloody strong," he said with a grimace. "We only have so much coffee on board—gotta make it stretch the entire voyage."

"Thank you, Captain. I'll remember that," she replied thinking, *He doesn't know a damn thing about good coffee. Next time he'll get a cup of tepid sea water.*

Dick nodded to a navigation table with a map stretched across it. "Put the plate there…but don't spill. Even with all this equipment, we still use a compass and a map."

Beth set the plate on the table and took a few steps across the wheelhouse to where Bert was at his post overlooking the winch and crane. She handed Bert his plate and whispered, "Is he always this hard to please?"

Bert lifted his right hand with its middle finger extended, as if that was its natural position. He pushed his glasses over his nose and offered a faint smile, revealing a set of teeth that reminded Beth of a box of Chicklets. "I wouldn't try too hard," he said in a voice just loud enough to be heard above the engines. "I've been with Captain Dick for three seasons, and once we're out to sea, I've never heard a complement."

"Lucky I've got tough skin," said Beth as she turned to leave the wheelhouse.

"Good for you," said Bert as he grabbed his plate. "Just a minute."

Beth watched as Bert inhaled his food. "You eat pancakes like a lizard eats a dragonfly," she said.

Bert squinted at Beth through his bottlecap glasses and handed her the empty plate. "Thanks," he belched. "Good grub."

Beth took the plate and smiled.

"That was the only way to eat a meal from our last cook," said Bert. "You didn't want to taste it. Yours deserves a little more respect."

"Thank you," said Beth.

As she backed down the steps, she glanced at the captain. He had grabbed a bottle of Johnnie Walker Scotch from a shelf beneath the steering wheel, pulled the cork from the bottle, and poured a healthy splash into his mug.

Hanta and Maggie were sitting next to each other on a pile of nets when Beth joined them on deck. The three of them settled into a comfortable position to eat their breakfast as seagulls dove and screamed above them. Crews of other ships waved to one another as they navigated the harbor—a maze of small gillnetters, long-line fishing boats, crab boats, and competing purse seiners. Most of the boats were still moored at their docks, and a couple of smaller boats were coming back into port. No one waved to the *Red Tempest*.

"What's that all about?" said Beth, as she shared her observation with the others.

Hanta looked at his plate and kept eating. Between mouthfuls of pancake he said, "Might have something to do with the accident last season."

"Captain Dick told us about the accident a couple of weeks ago," said Beth. "Were you friends with Siku?"

Hanta nodded. "He was my best friend."

Maggie gasped, "Oh no."

"Dick said Siku refused to replace a cable that was frayed," said Beth, "and that's why it snapped."

Hanta pointed to a shiny new cable spooled around a pully on the boom. "That's the cable, but it was the captain who was too cheap and too impatient to get it repaired before we left port."

"That's not the story we heard," said Maggie who had wiped the last bit of maple syrup from her plate with a fork full of pancakes.

"Siku found the frayed cable when he inspected the boat," said Hanta. "He told the captain that it needed to be replaced. He even ordered a new one, but it was a special order and wouldn't arrive until the following day. Captain Dick insisted on going out to sea. The Coho silvers were rumored to be running heavy, and our catch was short of last year's." Hanta put down his plate and looked up at the wheelhouse. "He's a greedy one—that Captain Dick—and a risk taker."

"Dick said that you were knocked unconscious, and he did everything he could to help your friend," said Beth.

"Ha," snorted Hanta. "Captain thought I was out cold, but I heard him shout, 'Forget that worthless Eskimo, Bert. Haul in that load of fish. We'll get to him after the catch is in the hold.' I tried to get up and help him myself, but that's when I blacked out."

"Siku had a wife and son?" said Beth. "How are they doing? Did they get the insurance money that was promised to them after the accident?"

"Siku's family got a small settlement," said Hanta, "but the courts awarded Captain Dick a pile of money because he lost the catch."

Hanta took a sip of coffee before he explained. "Several boats had come into the area to help after they heard that a man had been lost. I was transferred to another boat and taken back to Homer where they put a piece of tape on my chin and told me I had a concussion. It took a couple of days to find Siku's body. I heard that the crew of the *Red Tempest* finally pulled him out of the water in a net full of Coho. They had to sort him out like some kind of unwanted bycatch when they swept the Coho into the hold. Then the refrigeration unit failed. By the time they got back to Homer, the fish had spoiled in the hold."

"I'm surprised you'd ever want to work for Captain Dick again after that happened," said Beth.

Hanta offered a wan smile. "There's an old Inuit proverb that says, 'Those who know how to play can easily leap over the adversities of life.'"

Beth followed Hanta's gaze to the west. The ocean was a plate of glass with a trace of clouds sprouting from the horizon. "The ocean is certainly calm today," she said. "A great day for fishing." She collected the empty plates from the crew and took them back to the galley.

Captain Dick had turned on his autopilot and set the *Red Tempest* on a course for Cook Inlet. Promptly at 0800, he rang a bell to call everyone on deck. "All right mates," he said. "I've set a course for the best King salmon fishing in the world. It's up to me to find 'em. It'll be up to you to haul 'em in." He looked at Maggie and Beth. "We've got a couple of young bubs on board. Let's hope they're up to the task."

Bert held out a piece of paper that he had been rubbing nervously between his fingers while the captain had been speaking. "You might want to take a look at this, Captain."

Captain Dick glanced at the paper and mumbled, "This ought to keep the landlubbers at home. We'll have the Kings all to ourselves. Our hold will be full before the others leave the harbor." He crunched the paper and threw it into a waste basket. "On to the Gulf of Alaska!"

Hanta leaned next to Beth and whispered, "Another Inuit proverb: 'He that boasts of his own knowledge proclaims his ignorance.'"

Chapter 13
Whitefish, Montana

Max

It was the middle of May and the ski crowd had been replaced with summer tourists. Max was hunched over the books in the office of the *Hellroaring Saloon.*

"Jake!" Max called to the bartender who was standing outside his door. "I have a question."

Jake stepped into the cramped office and hitched up his jeans. "What's the problem?"

"I've been comparing the liquor inventory with the receipts," said Max who leaned back in his chair and rubbed his eyes. "Based on the number of drinks we've poured we should have a lot more inventory on hand."

"Are you sure about that?" asked Jake as he closed the door behind him.

"I've checked three times, and I come up with the same answer each time. We're short of inventory." Max swallowed. "Got any ideas how that could have happened, Jake?"

"Maybe you missed a delivery in your count," said Jake. "The liquor truck sometimes stops more than once a week."

"I don't think so. I tracked every delivery and counted the bottles myself—even pulled open the cases."

Jake narrowed his eyes. "Are you accusing me of giving out freebies and not recording the sale?"

"That would be one explanation," said Max. "Is that what you're doing?"

Jake folded his arms and stared at Max. "Why don't you take the afternoon off, Max? Go for a hike or invite Twila to lunch. We'll discuss this later."

Linda

Linda couldn't help herself. She had been in Whitefish for six weeks and *Lucky Lil's* was her favorite casino, a small establishment next to a gas station on the south edge of town. She had tried the *Bulldog Card Room* in the *Bulldog Saloon* soon after she had arrived. The décor was exciting, but it was filled with men who leered whenever she tried to get into a poker game. *Emerald City Casino*, south of *Lucky Lil's* on Highway 93 had tasty tacos, but she never came out ahead there. The previous week she had gotten lucky at *Lil's*. She walked out of the casino having netted a thousand dollars—ten crisp hundred-dollar bills.

I'm on a roll, she thought as she entered *Fab Fitness. Now's the time to head for Las Vegas where I can make some real money. Clint could come with me. I'll probably need a bodyguard and a porter when I walk out of Caesars Palace loaded with a suitcase full of bills.*

Linda had taken a job leading jazzercise classes three times a week at *Fab Fitness*, a club associated with the *Whitefish Lodge*. Over the years, the wall-length mirror in the fitness club had reflected all manner of human frailties, insecurities, and disappointments: Spandex stretched beyond its limit, dashed dreams of bodies that could never meet their owners' expectations, and dancers out of step with the music of life. But Linda had ignored the fat and flab of her clients and stoked their insatiable egos. She gave inspiring pep talks, piped in pounding rock music, and smiled broadly as she high-kicked her way from one class to the next.

As the jazzercise leader, Linda had been under the scrutiny of the mirror herself. Recently she had been plagued with artificial enthusiasm—imposter syndrome. *Am I losing it? I don't have the same bounce in my step. Is that a cellulite wrinkle under my leggings?*

As the music ended and she released her class, her phone buzzed on the table next to the mirror.

"Mom. This is Clyde."

"Hi, honey," said Linda. She wiped the sweat from her brow, hung her towel around her neck, and sat down on a chair next to the table. "What a pleasure to hear from you. How are you doing? How's the house? Everything okay?"

"I'm okay," said Clyde, "but I don't know if you are."

A trickle of sweat went down Linda's spine. "Why do you say that?"

"I just came from the post office. There was a certified letter to Dad—to Maxwell Wharton. No one uses that name unless it's really important. They let me sign for it since they knew I'm his son. I lied and told them Dad would be home from work later this afternoon, so I could give it to him as soon as he got there."

Linda asked, "Did you open it?"

"It's from the IRS." There was a pause at the end of the phone. In a low voice, Clyde finally said, "I was curious."

"What's in it?" demanded Linda. "We may as well find out what this is all about."

She waited as Clyde brought the letter to the phone.

"Well, get on with it. What does it say?"

Clyde replied slowly, "The heading says it's a 'Letter of Inquiry.'" He re-read the rest of the letter. "It says they want an explanation for some undeclared income and says that he is being investigated for tax fraud."

"Holy shit," said Linda. "That sounds serious…Does it say how much income he hasn't reported?"

"I don't know if this could be right, but could it be a hundred and fifty thousand dollars?"

"A hundred and fifty thousand! Why, that sonofabitch. I always wondered why we filed separate tax returns."

"I'm sorry you're caught in the middle of this, Clyde." Then she smiled to herself. "You did the right thing, honey. Can you send that letter to me?"

Linda turned off her phone and looked up. A pretty woman with blond hair and a noticeable birthmark was staring at her.

Chapter 14
The Red Tempest

Maggie

The *Red Tempest* had been traveling west for six hours. The Gulf of Alaska had turned the color of slate but remained as still as death. Earlier in the day, Maggie had seen a couple of seiners and a trawler going east, but she had seen no other fishing boats since they had left the harbor.

"There's a school of Kings!" shouted Dick from the wheelhouse. "All hands-on deck."

Bert settled into his position at the winch controls. Beth climbed into the skiff. Hanta and Maggie stood ready in the stern to play out the net and lines. The first set went exactly as it had during their training sets. In contrast to their practice runs, the purse seine was full of fish. When it was emptied, the deck was alive with King salmon. As soon as Hanta and Maggie swept the fish into the hold, a stiff breeze blew up from the southeast. The ribbon of clouds that had been on the horizon had grown into an ominous mountain of mist and sheets of rain. In the distance, six-foot swells topped with whitecaps suddenly appeared. Maggie began to feel sick to her stomach.

The other crew members had donned slickers and rubber boots in anticipation of the coming storm, but Maggie had been too hot and needed to change. She forced herself to go below deck where the acidic remainder of her lunch caught in her throat. She swallowed hard. As she held her breath and pulled her boots over her wool socks, she heard a commotion from the wheelhouse above her.

"You sure we shouldn't turn back, Captain?" shouted Bert. "Looks to me like the weather report was spot on."

"The hell with that weather report," cried Dick into a growing wind. "Prepare for a second set. You saw the size of that last catch."

Maggie climbed out of the cabin and remembered the scrap of paper Bert had handed to Captain Dick. She steadied herself and retrieved it from the trash:

A MAJOR STORM REMAINS ON TRACK TO BRING HEAVY RAIN AND STRONG WINDS TO MUCH OF THE SOUTHERN MAINLAND DURING THE EARLY TO MIDDLE PART OF THIS WEEK. SOUTHEASTERLY WIND GUSTS OF 65 TO 80 MPH ARE POSSIBLE FOR THE GULF OF ALASKA WITH WIDESPREAD GALE TO STORM FORCE WINDS

Good God, thought Maggie. *This sounds worse than a November gale on Lake Superior.*

She climbed out of the cabin and leaned over the side to throw up. The wind splattered bits of partially-digested lunch on her slicker. She wiped her mouth and climbed the ladder to the wheelhouse. Bert was seated at the winch control overlooking the stern of the ship.

Maggie held the crumpled paper in front of the captain. She shouted, "This looks serious, Dick. Are you sure we should be out here with this weather approaching?"

"It's *Captain* Dick," he said as the scar on his left eyebrow turned scarlet. "Remember? Once we leave the pier, this boat is not a democracy. The captain is in charge and I'm responsible for making weather decisions."

Maggie shrugged and turned to leave. Dick looked over his shoulder and added, "You look crook. Clean yourself up, for God's sake."

She looked at Bert. He simply lifted his middle finger in its usual solitary and upright position, waved it in the air, and turned away to focus on the job ahead.

Hanta braced himself on the stern deck doling out the cork line. Beth had already headed the skiff into the growing chop. Despite her intention to swing it into a wide arc, the wind pushed her in a straight line off the stern.

Maggie heard Dick shout at Bert, "Goddammit. Tell her to pull that bathtub of hers into an arc."

The seiner lurched forward sending Maggie to her knees. She scrambled to her feet. Having forgotten her nausea, she wobbled to the stern to help Hanta play out the net.

The skiff rose high above a swell and then dove out of sight when it fell between the waves. "This is crazy," shouted Maggie. "Will Beth be able to maneuver the skiff into position next to the boat?"

Hanta delivered a stoic reply. "Another Inuit proverb: 'It is an ill wind that blows nobody any good.'" He wiped the rain from his brow. "Even if Beth brings the skiff close to the ship, with all this bobbing up and down, most of the fish will have fallen out of the net before we can purse up."

Maggie watched the cork line stretch over the waves as the skiff labored to complete the circle. By now, the seiner was pitching in the waves. "Turn her into the wind, Captain," shouted Bert, "or we'll never keep her upright."

"Do as you're told," shouted Dick. "We're harvesting this catch."

Beth's skiff gradually approached the rocking seiner on its starboard side. The skiff was on the leeward side of the wind, but waves crashed over the port side of the seiner, sloshing seawater over the deck. Maggie and Hanta stood at the short railing on the starboard gunwale hoping to grab the cork and tow lines attached to the skiff.

Hanta waited as the ship rose to the crest of a wave and the skiff momentarily fell off to the other side. As the *Red Tempest* fell into the trough and the skiff slid toward the ship, Hanta reached for the cork line. He fumbled with the clasp and cursed. The skiff and trawler collided, crushing Hanta's hand. As the cork line floated away from the side of the ship, Hanta reached for it with his good hand. Just then the ship lurched, throwing Hanta off balance and into the ocean.

Maggie screamed, "Man overboard!" She knelt on the deck and stretched out her hand, but Hanta had already been swept out of reach.

Beth shouted from the skiff, "Maggie! Catch the tow line. Let me get Hanta."

Maggie stumbled to her feet and moved toward the stern.

Chapter 15
Whitefish, Montana

Linda

Linda was startled at the presence of the pretty young woman. She had appeared out of nowhere after her conversation with Clyde at the *Fab Fitness Center*.

"Hi," said the woman cheerfully. "I'm Twila. I know your husband."

Linda frowned and said, "I've seen you before. You're a clerk at *The Toggery*. I shop there from time to time…and I'm not surprised that you know my husband. I've seen you in the neighborhood where I'm staying."

"I've seen you before too," said Twila. "Max has pointed you out to me. My boyfriend, Phil, and I live in one of the cabins near yours—the one you share with that guy you hang out with— Clint is his name. Right?"

"Poor Phil," chided Linda, ignoring Twila's comment about Clint. "Is Phil aware that you slip into Max's cabin periodically. You're not the only one keeping track of the neighborhood."

"We have lunch together," said Twila, somewhat defensively.

"Ha, lunch," said Linda. "We used to call that a 'nooner.'"

Linda folded her arms and looked closely at the woman whose hands were trembling. "What can I do for you, Twila?"

Twila clutched her purse tightly. "I think there's something you should know about your boyfriend—woman to woman, that is."

"Oh? What's that?"

"You probably wonder how Clint earns his living?"

"He works construction jobs in the summer," said Linda. "He told me his boss called recently and he has to leave soon."

"He'll be leaving soon all right," smirked Twila. She was breathing fast and appeared nervous. "Clint comes here every winter. The lecherous fool hangs around the saloon looking for pretty co-eds. He can pick out the needy ones—those without a lot of self-confidence. Once he finds his mark, he tells her she can make a pile of money simply by taking off her clothes." Twila inhaled a calming breath and forced a smile. "He's Hollywood's most lucrative porn star recruiter."

Linda's face colored as she stood up and replied cynically. "How kind of you to keep me informed of the local gossip."

"Sorry, Linda. It's not gossip. Ask him yourself."

"Well, if that's the case, I doubt he would have recruited you," hissed Linda. "You wouldn't have made the cut. Look at you. Skinny as a rail. Birthmark on your neck. Rings under your eyes."

Twila sniffed, but replied quickly, "You'd be surprised what a dab of makeup and a strategically placed necklace can do. It was a few years ago but I was a celebrity. You can find me in a back-issue of *Penthouse*. They keep 'em in stock at the bookstore." As she turned to go, she added, "Also…I can assure you that the guys who are into that magazine are not interested in my neck."

Twila waved a dismissive hand and walked out.

Max

That night, Max received a call from Jake telling him that he wanted to meet with him at the *Hellroaring Saloon* before it opened. "Meet me here at ten. We've got a few things to discuss with you."

"I expect you do," said Max. "Have you figured out what happened to that missing liquor inventory?"

"We'll talk when you get here," said Jake gruffly.

The following morning Max was on his way to the saloon for his meeting with Jake when his phone buzzed. Linda was on the line. "A hundred and fifty thousand dollars?" she said. "Half of that is mine, you know."

Max had arrived at the bus stop and sat down on a stone wall that ran next to the sidewalk. "What are you talking about?"

"According to Clyde, you've gotten a certified letter from the IRS. Clyde signed for it on your behalf. He opened it and shared the contents with me. It sounds like you haven't reported all of our income." She paused to let her words take effect. "The IRS is on your ass, and I'm on your ass for not telling me about your lucrative moonlighting."

Oh shit, thought Max. *Something has gone wrong. Frankie was supposed to have taken care of this. A hundred and fifty thousand? There should be more than that. What the...?*

"I don't believe you, Linda," said Max in a hoarse voice. "I need to see that letter."

"I asked Clyde to send it to me. It ought to be here in the next day or so."

"I've got to make a few phone calls," said Max, calming slightly. "Then we should talk."

Linda sighed, "How can I ever trust you again, Max? But since we're finally being honest with each other and coming clean with our secrets, there's something *I've* been hiding from *you*."

"What now?"

"You might be happy to know that Clyde is not your son."

The bus arrived and opened the door for Max. He waved off the bus driver knowing that he'd be late for his meeting at the saloon.

"Of course, he's our son. Clyde and I may not have always gotten along, but I was there when he was born. I'm his father."

"Didn't you think it was strange that he has red hair? Yours is black. He's over six feet tall. You're only five eight. He's got brown eyes. You and I have blue eyes."

"That doesn't mean he's not mine. That's why we got married in such a rush. I wanted to be a responsible parent."

"You know Clint Gladley?"

"You mean that lanky cowboy you've been hanging around with?"

"He's Clyde's biological father. I'm surprised you haven't put two and two together before now. Clint and I had a relationship around the time when you and I met, but when I became pregnant you seemed like the one with the most potential." She paused to catch her breath. "Now this. I guess I was wrong. I can't believe you have the nerve to hide income from me—and the government."

"You selfish bitch," said Max. "I've always had my suspicions about Clyde's looks but thank you for confirming what I never wanted to believe."

"You're welcome," came Linda's cynical reply. "And enjoy your meeting with Jake. I expect he's already heard about your problems with the IRS."

The phone went dead as he was about to say, "Well, now Clyde will be your problem—and yours alone."

Max cleared his throat and speed-dialed Frankie Hillsborough.

"What the hell, Frankie?" said Max as soon as he answered. "I told you to file those voluntary disclosure papers. Now I find out that the IRS is pounding at my door and delivering certified letters to my son. What gives?"

"Oh damn, Max. There've been a lot of folks in the same position you are in."

"I'm sure not all of them are hiding income from their wives as well as the government," said Max acidly.

"You'd be surprised," chuckled Frankie, "but I've had to give priority to my bigger clients—mobsters, gangsters, politicians, and such—the sort that hire people to make death threats…and act on them if you don't respond pronto."

"What do I have to do to get to the top of your priority list, Frankie? Hire a hit man? Linda just read me the riot act and accused me of moonlighting. I wouldn't be surprised if she's got a contract on me already."

"It wouldn't be worth her while, Max. You've got no insurance. Tell you what. I'll file the voluntary disclosure immediately and back date it."

"Back dating government documents is risky business," fumed Max. "And another thing: Linda said there's only a hundred and fifty thousand at stake. There should be at least five hundred grand—and that's without any growth. You said the portfolio was lookin' good."

"Relax, Max. After I talked to you, I transferred a good share of your money into other accounts outside of Switzerland, so they should be harder to trace. The passwords and access information are in your password vault. I left the bonuses from the last three years in the Swiss account, so the government has something to find. The statute of limitations is only three years for taxes."

"I know about the statute of limitations," interrupted Max. "I'm a tax accountant, for God's sake. But the government can look back further if fraud is suspected."

"In the worst-case scenario," said Frankie, "the IRS will freeze the account they know about. They will figure the back taxes you owe, confiscate what they need, and return what's left."

"How much will that be?"

Max heard Frankie scribbling in the background. "I'd say you'd have enough left for a bicycle—or maybe a new set of skis."

"Ha! Good joke." Max scowled. "In that case, that's what I should tell Linda. I'd better explain it to her before she uses it as collateral for another gambling junket."

"Of course," Frankie added, "my fee will be in addition."

"Of course," sputtered Max. "I may need to sell the house."

"Max," said Frankie in a conciliatory tone. "You're in great shape. You're so cheap, you could dump that entire account and still have more money than you would know what to do with."

"Right."

Max hung up and worried. "*Fraud, back dating government documents, hidden accounts, jail time. Damn.*

The next bus pulled up to the curb and Max climbed aboard for the trip to the base of Whitefish Mountain. *Now, what do I tell Jake?*

Chapter 16
The Red Tempest

Beth

Beth stared into the driving rain. She coiled the tow line and heaved it toward Maggie's outstretched arms. "Damn," she shouted. "Missed."

The heavy clip on the end of the tow line fell into the ocean. "I'll try again," cried Beth as she re-coiled the rope. By now the skiff had drifted farther away from both Hanta and the ship. Beth made another attempt to fling the rope to Maggie. It fell short again.

"Forget it," called Beth. "I've got to get Hanta."

Maggie fell to her knees and pounded the railing. "Sorry, Beth. Sorry, Hanta."

Beth put the skiff into reverse and spoke into her microphone. "Bert, did you see where Hanta went down?"

"Last I saw, he was clinging to the cork line," said Bert, "but he's floating away from us fast."

In the radio headphone, Beth overheard Dick shouting to Bert in the wheelhouse. "Goddamn, worthless mates! Can't they do anything right? Bert, you take the wheel. I've got to go on deck to straighten out this dog's breakfast. Maneuver the *Tempest* to the end of the cork line, and I'll pluck it out of the water. We've still got a load of fish to catch."

"What about Hanta?" exclaimed Bert.

"It's his own damn fault for going overboard. What kind of a sailor is he anyway? Pick him up—but only when it's convenient."

Beth caught sight of Hanta flailing in the water in a fast drift away from her. She pushed on the throttle and sent the skiff in his direction. Suddenly, the engine sputtered and died.

"What happened now?" cried Beth.

A moment later, Bert returned to the radio. "I can barely see through my windshield," said Bert, "but it looks like your tow line is fouled on the prop. I've got to manage the *Tempest*. You sit tight, Beth. We'll pick you up after I've collected Hanta."

"The captain wants you to leave Hanta until after you've picked up the end of the cork line," said Beth. "He still thinks we can take in a catch."

"First things first," said Bert.

Beth tightened the hood around her face. A sheet of rain obstructed her view of the seiner. The skiff rolled over the waves perpendicular to the wind. She was drifting away—and fast. Her hands were numb, and her face burned from the icy rain. She turned the steering wheel and noticed that she had some control over her drift. The engine was useless, but the propeller and lower housing still acted like a rudder.

She turned the wheel to the left and began to drift slowly toward the cork line. Hanta still clung to the line, but he was hanging on near its far end and was barely moving. *If we don't get him soon, he'll die of hypothermia.* The yellow buoys inched closer to the skiff.

"Hang on, Hanta," she shouted. "I'm coming."

With a sharp turn of the wheel to the right, the stern of the skiff swung parallel to the cork line. The heavy buoys banged against the side of the skiff. Beth leaned over the side, and with a strength she didn't know she had, she pulled the line and top of the net into the boat. She worked her way to the bow of the skiff hand-over-hand. A tangled mass of buoys and net accumulated under her feet.

One foot, then two, then a yard. The wind helped her now as she gradually closed the distance to where Hanta had ceased to move at all. *Pull harder,* she told herself. *Pull harder.*

She glanced back at the *Red Tempest.* Dick was on the deck gesticulating wildly to Bert and shouting at Maggie. His cursing cut through the shrieking wind and banging cables. "Bloody hell! Damnit all...Worthless, f---ing crew."

Bert moved back and forth in the wheelhouse—first checking on Beth's progress, then staggering back to the steering wheel to keep the seiner on course. The *Tempest* was running with the wind. One end of the net and cork line trailed behind it attached to the boom. Beth and the skiff were attached to the net about three-quarters of the way along the cork line like a single pearl on a necklace. The loose end of the cork line bobbed in the distance with Hanta clinging to it.

A huge wave heaved the ship's bow into the air, then plunged it into the following trough. The *Tempest* scooped water over the deck, which nearly swept Maggie off her feet. A moment later the boat soared into the air again.

Beth, still wearing her radio headset, slowly made her way to Hanta's limp body. "Great job, Beth," said Bert. "Can you lift him on board the skiff?"

Beth was breathing hard. "I don't know," she panted. "I've used every ounce of strength just to get to him." She looked around the small vessel. "There's an oar tucked into the side of the gunwale," she said. "If Hanta has just a little strength left, maybe he can grab the oar and I can pull him out of the water. I can use it like a teeter-totter lever and at least get him to the edge of the boat where I might be able to roll him in."

"Atta girl," said Bert. "Afraid it's all up to you. I'm afraid of running over the purse line and fouling the seiner's prop. Then both of us will be dead in the water."

Beth dipped the handle of the oar over the edge and hollered instructions to Hanta. He lifted his glazed eyes and nodded as if he understood. Hanta grabbed the oar handle. Beth pulled him closer to the skiff and moved to the blade end of the oar. She pushed down with the entire weight of her body. Hanta came out of the water as far as his waste. "Now, reach for the gunwale," shouted Beth, "and I'll pull you in."

Hanta dropped the oar and grabbed for the side of the boat. The hand that had been crushed between the trawler and the skiff was useless, but his other hand folded over the wooden gunwale. Beth dropped the oar and lunged for Hanta's hand. She felt his cold knuckles. She squeezed his hand and reached for his arm. A wave rocked the boat. She lost her grip, and Hanta slipped back into the ocean.

"Oh no," cried Beth, as she watched Hanta sink below the surface.

She looked back at the big boat. Maggie was clutching the railing and wailed a long and desperate, "Noo…"

A wave caught the skiff and raised Beth and her little craft to a new height. Beth clung to the cork line hanging over the side of boat and waited for the wave to drop her closer to where Hanta had last been seen. Hanta's yellow slicker came into view. "Looks like he's caught in the net and is hanging onto it with his good hand," shouted Beth into the microphone.

Again, Beth dragged the cork line and net closer to Hanta. As the skiff dropped into the trough of the wave, the line slacked. Beth pulled with all her might and caught Hanta's arm. Just before the next wave sent the skiff soaring to its crest, Beth hauled Hanta's arm over the side. She pinned his arm to the inside of the boat and waited until the skiff plummeted again into the trough. She reached over the gunwale to grab the lower hem of Hanta's raincoat. The momentum of the boat allowed her to flop him over the side and into the boat. Hanta lay on the bottom of the boat. She could not tell if he was still breathing.

As Beth stared into Hanta's blue face, she felt the cork line and net unraveling off the stern of the skiff. She was floating away from the trawler again.

She squinted through the mist to see Bert sitting at the winch control. He had been watching her and now gave her further instructions. "You and Hanta must lay on top of the pile of buoys and netting that are on the bottom of the boat," he said. "That will hold the line in place so I can winch you back to the *Red Tempest*."

Beth did as Bert instructed.

As the skiff moved slowly toward the *Tempest*, she knelt over Hanta and heard Maggie scream, "Is he okay? He needs mouth to mouth!"

Beth waved and did as Maggie instructed.

Chapter 17
Whitefish, Montana

Max

The *Hellroaring Saloon* had opened for business as Max walked up to the bar.

"You're late," said Jake. "I told you ten o'clock." He looked at his watch. "It's damn near eleven."

"Missed the bus," said Max.

Jake looked around the bar. "Not much business yet. Come into the office and have a seat."

"I'd rather stand, if you don't mind," said Max as he closed the door behind him. *I may need to make a fast exit.*

Twila was also there waiting for him. "Hello, Twila," he said in surprise. "I'm confused. I didn't think this business meeting pertained to you."

"Oh, I think it might," said Twila.

"Max says our inventory is off," said Jake to Twila, explaining the purpose of the meeting. "I'm suggesting that he carefully recount before he submits his quarterly report."

"I think that would be a good idea," agreed Twila.

Max gave her a questioning look. "Why's that?"

"Jake and I have a little business venture that we'd like to protect," said Twila, "and we need your cooperation to keep it solvent."

"What kind of business are you talking about?"

"Let's just say we're doing a little bartering," said Jake. "It's a small operation, but one that means a lot to us. You really don't need any more details than that."

Before Max could ask any more questions, Twila added, "At my last visit to your cabin, I overheard you talking to a guy named Frankie. You said something like, 'Frankie, you can't tell Linda about this.'"

"I don't follow," said Max.

"I was getting out of the shower after our noon 'lunch' meeting," said Twila. "I must have surprised you, because you disconnected as soon as I peeked out the door."

Max paused, embarrassed. "He's just an old friend."

"Sounds to me like your wife doesn't know about this old friend of yours—and you don't want her to."

How much did Twila hear of that conversation? thought Max. *Did I say anything about my unreported income?*

"You're right," said Max. "It would be better if you didn't talk to Linda about Frankie."

"I've also been taking a class from your wife at the *Fab Fitness Center*," continued Twila, "and I overheard another phone conversation."

Good God. What now?

"Linda had been talking to her son—something about you and the IRS?"

"That's nothing," said Max. "I'm sure it's all a misunderstanding."

"I tell you what," said Twila, who looked at Jake. "We promise not to tell Linda about Frankie—and no one else about your run-in with the IRS—if you agree to cooperate with our little scheme."

"Now," said Jake with renewed confidence, "would you care to re-count that inventory one more time before you fill out your report?"

Max looked at Twila. "I suppose you don't want me to tell Phil about our little mid-day dalliances either."

Twila shrugged. "Tell him whatever you want. Like I told you before, he's got plenty of girlfriends."

Max closed his eyes and shook his head in disgust. "Where's that report?"

He signed off on the amended inventory values and handed it to Jake.

"Thanks, buddy," said Jake.

Max got up to leave. Twila asked him, "Care to have a drink? It's on the house."

"No thanks," said Max. He left the office and walked into the bar. He recognized *The Animals* on the juke box: *We Gotta Get Outa' This Place.*

"I couldn't agree more," muttered Max.

Linda

The morning after Linda's conversation with Twila, Linda lay in bed wrapped in Clint's arms.

"Mornin' babe," said Clint. "What a night, huh?"

Linda eased off Clint's chest and rolled to her back. "Yeah. Seems to get better and better."

She clasped her hands behind her head and stared at the ceiling. "Clint?"

"Yeah?"

"I thought your boss was expecting you soon. It's almost June. Construction work must have begun by now."

"Aw, the boss can do without me for a while. Besides, how could I pass up another night with you?" He rolled over and kissed her on the lips.

She pushed him away gently and said, "Someone just told me that your real job was recruiting young women to pose naked for magazines."

Clint leaned on an elbow and asked, "Who told you that?"

"Twila—one of our neighbors—that skinny gal who works at *The Toggery.* She said you recruited her. I didn't believe her."

Linda leaned on her side to face Clint. "She told me to look her up in *Penthouse.* I stopped in at the bookstore—the one with an adult section way in the back. I found the one she was referring to—an old February copy. I told the clerk I was buying it for my husband, which wasn't far from the truth. I opened it as soon as I got into the parking lot. There she was—the centerfold special."

"Twila, Twila, Twila," mused Clint. "She's right. I gave her the opportunity of a lifetime. She could have been an A-list porn star...but she blew it."

"Twila is right? You got her that job?"

"Pretty good gig," said Clint nonchalantly, "if you want me to be honest—good money in finding fees."

Linda sat up and pulled the sheets over her chest. "What do you mean, 'She blew it?'"

"Haven't you noticed the way she acts? Always sniffing. Jittery half the time. Rings under her eyes. She's not losing weight from working out."

"What?" asked Linda. "Is she on cocaine?"

"Full-fledged coke head," said Clint. "That boyfriend of hers—Phil? He's the local dealer. Jake and Twila are addicts who barter for their fixes. Jake trades free drinks for Phil and his pals. Twila trades sex for hers."

"Oh my God," said Linda. "That explains a lot."

"I recruited Twila about ten years ago. I bought her a ticket to L.A. with a damn good reference. She got the job at *Penthouse* plus a few more offers. Then she started using…maybe she couldn't handle the job expectations…maybe she started feeling guilty…I don't know…lost track of her for a while. I heard she got herself into treatment a couple of times. When she came back to Whitefish, she was clean. Then she met Phil and picked up the habit again."

"Are you still in the business of recruiting porn stars?" asked Linda.

"Only if I find a real knockout." He gave Linda a knowing smile.

"No…Clint. You said that no one but us would ever see those videos."

"No one has…so far." He clicked on the video screen. "Here's our last recording They're pretty good, if you ask me—and I'm a pro."

Linda leaned back and studied the screen. "Yeah. We *do* look pretty good. Can we make good money selling stuff like this?"

Clint laughed. "Great money…and it's fun work. Don't you think?"

"What if Clyde sees those videos? I wouldn't want them leaked onto the internet."

Clint snickered and gave her a hug. "That's very unlikely. I've got a new market."

Chapter 18
The Red Tempest

Maggie

Maggie's stomach churned as she clung to the railing next to the wheelhouse ladder. The *Red Tempest* rolled and pitched in the storm. Out in the skiff, Beth had managed to haul Hanta on board. The skiff was slowly being towed toward the ship by the cork line winch.

"Get to your post," barked Captain Dick who had joined Maggie on the deck. "Bert is almost in position to pick up the far end of the cork line." He pointed to the end of a line of yellow buoys that trailed beyond the skiff. "You see it there?"

"The weather is too rough," shouted Maggie into the wind. "You don't expect to land a net full of fish in these waves?"

"Damn right, I do," shouted Dick. "That net's full of Kings. I told Bert to let Beth drift free after she fouled the tow line. She knows we'll pick her up after we pull in the catch."

"But we won't have the skiff to pull against the other side of the ship," argued Maggie. "Won't we tip over?"

"Bert's a True Blue. I've seen him land a big haul many times without the skiff as a counterbalance."

"But what about Hanta?" wailed Maggie. "Beth made a heroic rescue, but we need to get them aboard first. I hope he's okay."

"Shut up and forget Hanta," cried Dick in exasperation. "There's always another Eskimo in need of work."

The bow of the seiner had reached the end of the cork line. "That's it, Bert," shouted Dick to the wheelhouse. "Now turn to port and pull alongside so Maggie can pick it up and attach it to the side of the ship."

The *Tempest* rocked violently from side to side as Bert maneuvered the trawler parallel to the wind. Maggie wretched. Nothing but bile stuck in her throat.

"Oh, for God's sake," barked Dick. "Do I have to do everything? Let me get the damn line myself." He knelt over the leeward gunwale and reached for the cork line.

Maggie lifted her head in time to see a tsunami sized wave approaching the boat on its windward side—a wave bigger than any they had experienced.

"Bert!" she cried. "Turn into the wind. That one's sure to capsize us."

Bert glanced at Dick, then at the menacing wave. Bert gunned the engine and turned hard into the wind. The seiner jumped in response, spinning the bow at a forty-five-degree angle into the wave. The *Tempest* creaked as it rode the wave to the top of the crest. Bert looked over his shoulder to the starboard deck. Captain Dick was nowhere to be seen.

"Dick fell overboard!" shouted Maggie.

Maggie

The storm passed as quickly as it had arrived. The sky cleared to a crystal blue with the Chugach Mountains silhouetted against the horizon. The wind and whitecaps had retreated to the west. The *Red Tempest* rolled in six-foot waves, but gently now. Maggie was on deck and Bert had returned to the wheelhouse.

"I couldn't help Dick when he fell overboard," lamented Maggie to Bert through an open window, "but I managed to grab the cork and purse line."

"Well done," said Bert. "Let's bring in the lines. I'll try to time the winch with the waves, so we don't list too far. Forget gathering the purse line, Maggie. We'll worry about untangling it later. Go to the stern and collect the net. Help Beth when the skiff approaches the ship."

Bert called Beth on the radio. "How is Hanta? Is he coming to?"

"He coughed and threw up as soon as I started mouth-to-mouth," said Beth. "Now he's cold as a fish and shaking uncontrollably. I'm sure he's got hypothermia. We've got to get him out of these wet clothes."

"I'm drawing in the cork line with the skiff attached," shouted Bert. "We'll get you on board asap."

Bert set the autopilot on a course directly into the waves and pulled the throttle back to a slow troll. Then he returned to the winch control and drew the lines over the power block.

"I think I saw Dick!" shouted Maggie. She pointed to the far side of the cork line arc. "I saw his slicker on the surface for a moment. Then I lost it again."

"You take care of Beth and the skiff," said Bert. "As soon as the purse line is taught, I'll come down on deck to help."

The skiff's bow touched the stern of the *Red Tempest*. Bert stopped the winch for the cork line but continued to collect the purse line on the deck. Maggie clipped a cable onto the skiff to secure it to the seiner and climbed aboard over the pile of netting to help Beth.

"I don't know if I can lift him again," gasped Beth.

"Outa' the way. Lemme do this." said Maggie. She bent over Hanta's limp body, took hold of one of his arms, and flung him over her shoulder in a fireman's carry. "You go ahead of me and open the door to the cabin."

Beth stayed on deck while Maggie took Hanta below and placed him gently on a lower bunk. Her hands were numb. After struggling to unbutton Hanta's soggy shirt, she took hold of the lapels of his shirt and ripped savagely. Buttons clattered off the walls and floor. She turned Hanta on his side and pulled his shirt from one arm, then the other. Then she slid off his trousers and wet socks. After rolling him into a couple of wool blankets, she kissed him on the forehead and went back on deck.

The purse line ground to a halt when it snugged tightly next to the trawler. The cork line was now free from the skiff, so Bert swung the boom over the starboard side of the transom and drew the net close to the ship. The purse net was boiling with King salmon and the ship listed dangerously in the pitch of a wave.

Beth looked up to the wheelhouse. "Release the damn fish," she shouted. "We're all going overboard again."

Bert called back, "I'm not worried about the fish, but I think the captain is in the net."

The winches had gone silent, and Bert appeared on deck with the others. The trawler was still in gear and dragged the distended purse seine along its starboard deck. Bert had returned the boom to its position over the stern, but the *Red Tempest* continued to rock perilously with every swell.

"There he is," cried Bert. He grabbed a long gaff hook that had been hanging on the side of the seiner and extended it toward Dick's yellow slicker. He pulled the body next to the ship. "Come over here, Maggie. Help me haul him on deck."

The ship dropped into a deep trough in a wave. Bert held onto the gaff hook pole with one hand and the railing with another. Maggie slipped on the deck but slid next to Bert at the gunwale. Beth was next to them and held Maggie's arm. Bert and Maggie reached over the side and pulled the captain aboard.

Dick's face was grey and swollen. The scar over his left eye had lost its anger leaving him with a resigned expression.

Maggie stared at him as he lay on the deck. "He was so kind on land. What made him become such an asshole as soon as he took control of his boat?"

Bert pushed his glasses on his nose. "I don't know. Greed? Pride?"

"He was really no better than Ridley," said Maggie. "I should have seen it earlier."

Beth gave her friend a reassuring hug and asked, "What should we do with him?"

"There will be an inquiry," said Bert. "We'll need to keep him cold for the autopsy."

The three of them looked at one another and then at the hatch on the deck.

"Yes," Bert nodded. "The hold is chilled."

"Into the hold—along with the fish?" he asked.

"Agreed. Into the hold…"

Chapter 19
Homer, Alaska

Beth

It had been a peaceful month for Beth who had been the lone resident on the *Red Tempest* since their ill-fated fishing voyage. Beth needed lodging, so she remained on board with her espresso machine and computer. Bert had returned to his apartment in Homer. Hanta had been hospitalized for a week, and having no family in Homer, was released into Maggie's care. Maggie stayed with Hanta at a local hotel to assist him in his convalescence from hypothermia and multiple metacarpal fractures.

On a sunny afternoon in late June, Bert, Maggie, and Hanta joined Beth on deck for a crew reunion. Beth served fresh coffee to Bert and Hanta, then poured the last of Dick's Black Label Scotch into a mug for Maggie. They toasted their survival as they discussed the events surrounding their return to port.

The *Red Tempest* had chugged slowly into Homer the morning after the storm. The same fleet of purse seiners, small gillnetters, long-line fishing boats, and crab boats that had remained in port because of the threat of bad weather were preparing to depart.

Beth, Maggie, and Bert had pulled the captain's body from the hold a half hour before they entered the harbor. They sorted him from the King salmon, hosed off the slime, and laid him on the deck with a token measure of respect.

Bert had radioed ahead and explained their situation. Flashing lights and a squad of officials met them at the dock. The medics first checked Captain Dick for vital signs. He smelled like a relative who had overstayed his visit. Finding no pulse, no heartbeat, and no pupillary response, the first responders directed their attention to Hanta. They quickly loaded him onto a stretcher and into a waiting ambulance. Maggie accompanied him to the hospital to give the emergency room staff the full history of what had happened.

The coroner determined that the official cause of death for Captain Richard Fleshman was drowning, but that his death was complicated by a blood alcohol content of 0.16 percent—twice the legal limit. Armed with that knowledge, a very rudimentary investigation by the Coast Guard followed. The summary of their inquiry: Captain Fleshman's death was an act of God.

"I've enjoyed staying here on the boat," said Beth. "The only inconvenience has been a steady stream of worried creditors: the bank that holds the mortgage on the *Red Tempest*, the hardware store, the liquor store, and the owner of *AJ's*—for Dick's overdue bar bill. He was even overdue at the library. It seems that every business in town offers credit to the locals over the winter— regardless of their credit rating. They expect the accounts will be settled after the first catch of the season."

"We dropped our first catch at the processing plant after the ambulance left," said Bert. "Even though it was a big catch, I doubt it will begin to cover all his debts."

"That's for sure," said Bert. "And Dick told me he hadn't filed his tax returns the last couple of years either."

"You're right," said Beth. "Furthermore, the captain left no will, and his only heirs are an estranged brother and a more-estranged ex-wife who apparently lent him some money for the fishing business just to get him to leave town. They are both from Perth, Australia. His ex is deciding if it will be worth the time and expense to pursue recovering her loss. The county was forced to deal with Dick's remains."

"What a mess," said Maggie.

"Dick's debts are really no concern of ours," said Bert cheerfully, "but I'm still in need of a job."

"Me too," said Hanta, "but my hand won't be healed up for at least six weeks—maybe longer."

The group sat quietly and sipped their drinks.

"Do you think you could captain a boat, Hanta?" asked Bert. "Maybe this is our chance to start a business of our own."

"You mean, me captain the *Red Tempest*?" said Hanta.

"Yeah. Form a partnership," said Bert. "What do you think?"

"The bank would welcome a buyer who could assume the loan on the boat," said Beth, "but there might even be more liens that we don't know about."

"We'd need a loan and a good accountant," said Hanta, "—someone to sort out Dick's estate and to help set up a business."

"We'd definitely need a business manager," said Bert. "I'm good with math and mechanics, but if you put a dollar sign in front of a number, I'm certain to lose it all."

Beth smiled and said to Maggie, "Remember Max?"

"That guy on the train?"

"Yeah. He was an accountant."

"What a hunk," said Maggie. "Oops. Sorry, Hanta. No offense."

"You mean like that hunk, Captain Dick?" chided Hanta.

Maggie blushed for the first time that Beth could remember.

"I'm a little impulsive when it comes to men," Maggie admitted.

"As I recall," said Beth, "Max's wife didn't think he was that much of a hunk."

"No," agreed Maggie. "She was a piece of work—Linda. Wasn't that her name? I wonder what happened to them?

"We're getting a little ahead of ourselves," said Hanta. "We'll need a loan, but no one will finance us without a downpayment—particularly to an indigenous like me."

"I've got a few bucks tucked away," said Bert. "We could use that as a start."

"I don't have much," said Hanta, "but I'd be willing to contribute plenty of sweat equity."

"I'll check my bank account in Two Harbors," said Maggie. "I've got some savings in my name that I'd be willin' to contribute. Count me in."

"You were seasick the whole time we were out," said Hanta. "You sure about this?"

"That was a terrible storm," said Maggie. "Besides, they've got drugs for that sort of thing. Next time I'll be better prepared."

She looked at her friends. "Guess I'm impulsive about my business decisions too."

They all laughed.

"What about you, Beth?" said Maggie. "How'd you or Lance Freeport like to become partners in a fishing venture?"

Beth shook her head and said, "Lance still has a book to finish, and his deadline is closing in…but I could help out as your skiff man until you can find a replacement."

"That means we'd only need one other deck hand to fill out our crew," said Hanta. "We might miss the King salmon run, but if we get our act together, we can be ready for the Coho run."

"Do you know how to get a hold of Max?" asked Maggie.

"I saw the logo on his shirt—*Henderson Accounting*," said Beth. "I can track him down on the internet."

Chapter 20
Whitefish, Montana

Max

Max returned to his cabin and placed a call to Frankie Hillsborough.

"Frankie?"

"Hello, Max." Before Max could say another word, Frankie said, "Stop your worrying. I sent the letter to the IRS and backdated it like we talked about earlier. Everything is in the works."

"That's good, Frankie, because I'd like you to make a few withdrawals from those non-Swiss accounts you set up. Life is too short to let that money go unused."

"No problem, Max. Tell me how much you'd like withdrawn, and I'll wire it this afternoon."

Max placed his order for the wire transfers, then said, "There's one more thing."

"What's that?"

"I need you to draft a letter for me. Address it to Linda Wharton, and send a copy to Clyde Wharton, who apparently is no longer my son."

Max tapped his phone to disconnect from Frankie. A moment later someone else was calling: Unknown number.

"Hello?"

Linda

Linda arrived at the Whitefish Post Office when it opened at ten a.m. It was a modern building with a blue awning located a block north of Riverside Park. Linda signed for the certified letter and walked around the corner to the parking lot in front of the attached fire station. She tore open the envelope:

Dear Ms. Wharton:

You are hereby advised that your husband, Maxwell Wharton, has asked me to file divorce proceedings on his behalf.

Enclosed is a cashier's check for $75,000, your half of the income mentioned in the letter from the IRS. Maxwell's explanation is that it was set up as a savings account to protect it from your gambling addiction. By cashing this check, you acknowledge full compensation from this account.

Maxwell also suggests that with your consent, you sell the house in Minnesota and distribute the net proceeds three ways: one-third to you, one-third to your son, Clyde, and one-third to Maxwell.

Official documents to follow in certified post.

Sincerely,
Franklin Hillsborough
Attorney at Law   cc: Clyde Wharton

Gambling addiction? That's a bunch of B.S. thought Linda. *I win more than I lose. That makes me a professional gambler, not an addict.*

I wonder if I should cash the check. There might be more, but then I'd probably have to share it with a damn lawyer. I'll talk it over with Clint.

Max

Max held the phone closer to his ear and repeated, "Hello? Who is this?"

"Hello, Max," said a voice that he did not recognize. "This is Beth Lancer. We had dinner on the train several months ago."

"Oh yes. Sorry, I vaguely remember you, but I do remember that outspoken redhead who was also at our table."

Beth laughed. "Yes," she said. "That was Maggie. She and I are in Homer, Alaska."

"Homer, Alaska! What in the world drew the two of you to that distant outpost?"

"It's a fish tale, and a good one. The reason I'm calling is that we find ourselves in need of an accountant. I tracked you down from the logo on your shirt. When I called *Henderson Accounting*, they said you had quit but they were kind enough to give me your phone number."

"What can I do for you?" said Max. "It just so happens that I am currently unemployed."

"Would you like to come to Alaska? I can tell you the whole story."

Max considered the proposal for exactly thirty seconds. "I'll make my travel arrangements and call you when I get to Homer."

Linda

A second letter awaited Linda when she returned from the post office. This one was handwritten in an envelope on the front step of the cabin she shared with Clint. She picked it up and walked into the cabin. Clint was sitting at the table fiddling with his Sam Elliot mustache, nursing a Black Butte Porter, and puffing on a fresh Montecristo.

"Did you know this letter was on our doorstep?" asked Linda.

"News to me," said Clint. "Just got up."

Linda waved the certified letter in the air. "I need your advice. Read this." She handed Clint the letter from the post office while she tore open the letter she had discovered on the step:

Dear Linda,

I expect you have read the letter from my attorney. I encourage you to accept the terms I laid out for you. The IRS is serious about its claims on the savings account. I may have to disappear for a while until things get sorted.

Please give my regards to Clyde. Tell him that I care for him and wish him the best. I'll track him down sooner or later and renew our relationship as adults. Give him a bit of advice on my behalf: Choose your friends and lovers carefully.

Sincerely,
Max

She looked up. "I don't think I need your advice anymore, Clint. I'm going to accept the cashier's check." She looked at him with a broad smile. "I'm rich!"

She crumpled the note from Max and threw it in the wastebasket, then walked over to Clint and gave him a hug. "Let's go to Vegas," she said. "I'm tired of Whitefish."

Clint put down his cigar and pulled her into his lap. "What about Los Angeles?"

"I'm feeling lucky. L.A. can wait."

Chapter 21
Homer, Alaska

Max

Max took the train from Whitefish to Seattle, then a taxi to the waterfront where he peeled twelve hundred-dollar bills from his roll of cash and paid for a ticket on a freighter from Seattle to Anchorage. He was one of only four passengers on board, which suited him fine—no need for a lot of conversation. He ate with the crew, lounged on the deck, and inhaled the fresh sea air. Life aboard ship was agreeable to him.

Ten days later he arrived in Anchorage. The southbound AK Bus to Homer departed at two p.m. from Ted Stevens International Airport outside the Alaska Airlines baggage claim. His taxi delivered him in time to purchase a one-way ticket. He bought lunch at the first stop—Coast Pizza in Girdwood, stayed on the bus in Cooper Landing, sipped a latte from Starbucks in Soldotna, and arrived at the Aspen Suites Hotel in Homer at seven p.m. where he booked the last available room.

The following morning, he called Beth Lancer. "I'm in town and I'm looking forward to seeing you, Maggie, and meeting your new friends."

"How about *AJ's OldTown Steakhouse and Tavern* for dinner tonight?" suggested Beth. "I can tell you our story and introduce you to the entire crew."

"I'm sure I can find it," said Max. "Six-thirty?"

"Perfect."

Max arrived a few minutes early, took a seat at the bar, and ordered a *Bud Light*. Beth walked in a few minutes later, followed by Maggie, a slightly-built Inuit with a bandage on his right hand, and a short man with a pug nose.

"Hello, Max," said Beth. "Thanks for coming." She was tanned and appeared more self-assured than Max had remembered from their brief encounter on the train.

"Eh, handsome!" shouted Maggie, whose cleavage was pink with sunburn. She pushed Beth aside to shake Max's hand. "Welcome to Homer. Hope you're as good an accountant as Beth here says you are." Still gripping Max's hand, she looked toward Beth. "She checked The Google. It says a lotta good things 'bout you."

Max smiled modestly and said, "I had one client who really liked my work—but I'm tired of the stress. I'm looking for something new."

"We've got just the thing for you," said Beth, "but first, you need to meet the rest of our crew members. "This is Bert. He's the ship's engineer, and the one who crewed with our previous captain longer than anyone else. We'll tell you more about him later."

Bert pushed his glasses up his nose using his index finger for a change and extended a welcoming hand to Max. "Nice to meet you."

"And this is Hanta," continued Beth. "He is a deckhand who taught Maggie all about purse seining."

Hanta extended his left hand to Max. "Sorry. Got my hand in a place where it shouldn't have been."

"He had it comin'," chuckled Maggie.

Hanta frowned at Maggie and explained, "An accident at sea."

"Let's have a seat," said Beth, "and we'll tell you all about it."

Maggie pointed to the booth she and the captain used to reserve. "Since Captain Dick will be the main attraction today, let's sit there."

The waitress arrived to take their orders. "I'll have a Johnnie Walker Black Label Scotch," said Maggie..."in Dick's honor."

Beth ordered a coffee with cream. Hanta ordered iced tea, Bert an Alaskan Amber, and Max another Bud Light. As they sipped their drinks, the group shared the story of how they were hired by Captain Richard Fleshman to crew the *Red Tempest*, and how their first voyage ended in a near disaster for all of them.

"I don't feel too bad for the selfish sonofabitch," said Bert, "but I wish he hadn't left his affairs in such a mess."

"It sounds like he owes money to everybody in town," said Maggie.

"And he didn't file his taxes the last couple of years," continued Hanta.

Max listened patiently, then explained, "I'm a tax accountant and was able to save that client of mine a pile of money. I think I can help you out of this mess, but I can't sign my name to any of the documents. I can offer advice, but someone else will have to submit the paperwork."

"Why's that?" asked Maggie.

"Personal issues," said Max.

"Your wife?"

"Close enough."

"It's really none of our business," said Bert. He took a sip of beer and continued, "I don't have a lot of respect for Dick, but he probably trusted me more than anyone else in town. I'll go to the bank and offer to manage his estate. Maybe we can get his ex to sign off on her claim to any of his assets."

"When she learns that there are more liabilities than assets," said Max, "I don't think that will be a problem," He thought a moment and added, "When you go to the bank, ask them if you could rent the *Red Tempest* for the rest of the season while we get this straightened out. They might be eager to generate some income while they find a buyer."

"We're still short a deckhand," said Hanta. "I checked with all of the locals, and they're already booked on other boats."

"What about you, Max?" said Bert. "How'd you like to become a deckhand?"

"Afraid I need to make myself scarce for the next month or so," said Max. "I've got a few issues to sort out too."

"There's no better place to make oneself scarce than the Gulf of Alaska," said Maggie. "You could be my 'prentice."

Hanta laughed. "One cruise and she's an expert. Remember, I'll be the captain this time around."

"I enjoyed the cruise on the freighter from Seattle," said Max. "I think some fresh air would do me good, but won't we still have to register my name as a member of the crew?"

"Let's give you a new name for the ship's roster," suggested Beth. "How about Rowdy Limburg? It's got a nice ring to it, don't you thnk?"

"Hmm. I like it," said Max. "Let's go fishing."

Chapter 22
Las Vegas, Nevada

Linda

Linda had never been to Las Vegas. In the early morning hours at the cabin in Whitefish, she lay in bed and imagined walking into Caesars Palace—the Holy Grail of gambling, the epitome of poker, the Superman of slots, the Everest of roulette, the Titanic of luxury.

She woke Clint with a nudge to his shoulder. "Wake up, Clint. It's time to go shopping."

Clint groaned. "Nothing's open 'til ten."

"Coffee first, then," she said, and leapt out of bed.

Linda and Clint arrived at the *Toggery* at one minute after ten. She tried on a dark pair of dress slacks and a white silk blouse. "I'll take this and the same combo with navy blue slacks and a powder blue blouse."

Next, she modeled a black cocktail dress that came halfway up her thigh, a red silk scarf, and a matching pair of red stiletto heels. She did a graceful pirouette. "What do you think, Clint? Will this do for starters?"

"You got *my* attention," said Clint. "How long do you expect me to let you wear that getup before I tear it off ?"

"You're very sweet," said Linda, "but if I'm going to be a high roller, I need to look the part."

"Don't you worry, babe. You look like a high roller to me. You'll get their attention the minute you walk into the casino."

"That," laughed Linda, "and a purse full of money will get their attention."

She ran the scarf through her fingers. "This is my lucky charm. I can feel it."

She paid her bill and said, "Now Clint, we need to get you a nice suit."

"You think a new seta duds'll matter one way or the other?"

"There's a dress code at Caesars Palace," said Linda. "I don't want you lookin' like a country bumpkin." She spread her arms in a welcoming gesture, "especially when I look like this."

"As you wish, my dear," said Clint. "I suppose the *Chill Clothing Company* is the only place in town that might have a suit."

"That'll be our next stop."

The following morning, Linda and Clint left Whitefish for Glacier Park International Airport, just 19 miles southeast of the resort. They boarded a direct flight for Sin City. By mid-afternoon, they were standing on the blistering tarmac of Harry Reid International Airport.

"Isn't his exciting?" said Linda. "I can't wait to get to the casino."

"You won't have to wait long," said Clint. "I hear the bells and whistles of a one-armed bandit right inside the terminal."

While they waited for their luggage, Linda dropped a few silver dollars into a slot machine. Bells rang and lights flashed as the slot machine paid out a jackpot.

"See?" exclaimed Linda. "I own this place."

As soon as their bags arrived, Linda ran into the restroom and changed into her glamor garb. When she returned to the terminal, she told Clint to do the same. "We need to make an entrance. I'll order a limo while you get changed. It won't do to show up at Caesars in a Yellow Cab."

A half hour later a limousine that could have passed for a hearse pulled up at the curb. A uniformed chauffeur stepped out to hold the door and load their bags. The Las Vegas skyline was etched against the Spring Mountains in the west while the flat and desolate Mojave Desert spread out to the east. The limo drove them north on Wayne Newton Boulevard and merged onto Paradise Road, then turned left onto East Flamingo Road. On Las Vegas Boulevard, they passed the Julius Caesar statue. A half-dozen young men in dark suits, sunglasses and boutonnieres posed in cocky postures in Juno Garden. An equal number of bridesmaids dressed in pale green stood next to them. The bride and groom, both dressed in white, wore forced smiles.

The limo rolled over inlaid tile as it circled an emerald fountain. Its centerpiece was three curly-headed, muscular, nude wrestlers competing to reach for a cloud in a cloudless sky. A circular balustrade surrounded the fountain. On top of the balustrade, statues of two Roman warriors fought to control their rearing white stallions.

"Looks like the horses are frightened of the water," said Clint.

"Shh," said Linda, as she straightened her skirt. "We're here."

The limo stopped below a massive canopy at Porte Cochere. The chauffeur opened the door and within moments, two bellboys stood at attention next to him. They had their bags in hand before Linda placed a foot on the marble sidewalk. She smiled in anticipation of the ogling tourists.

Clint stepped out after her, stretched his legs, and followed her to the front desk. As soon as they checked in, the bellboys whisked the bags to their room. Clint followed them to the room while Linda went directly to the casino cashier. She deposited $75,000.

Linda had to choose from 1,324 slot machines to warm up. She had heard that the larger denomination slots gave better odds at a win, so she took a few pulls at the hundred-dollar *Mega Joker*, then moved to *Blood Suckers*. By dinnertime she broke even with a winner on the *Starmania* slots.

Linda made a reservation for dinner with Clint at *Restaurant Guy Savoy*. Linda ordered the 5 Star Celebration Menu for each of them at $395 per person. She drew the line at an option that included the premium wine pairing at $650 a head. "I don't want to get spoiled this early in the trip," she explained to Clint who had come to dinner underdressed. He had to run to *Ted Baker London* to purchase a hundred-dollar tie to meet the restaurant's dress code.

The celebration menu included several items that they recognized: octopus, caviar, and watermelon; several that they thought they recognized: artichoke and black truffle soup, A5 Japanese Wagyu Beef, lobster, ravioli, and Autour du Chocolat; and several that required a French interpreter (which they were too proud to request): Daurade, Fava, Coral Jus - Tête de Moine, and Confiture.

Still not satiated with her first day in Vegas, Linda threw a handful of $500 tokens into the *White Rabbit Megaways* slot machine—and hit a five-thousand-dollar jackpot.

"I knew it!" shouted Linda. "I've found my purpose in life."

Chapter 23
The Red Tempest

Maggie

It was the middle of August, and the ocean rippled with whitecaps. Maggie sat next to Hanta in the wheelhouse as he navigated the *Red Tempest* to the Coho fishing grounds. "You said you don't have family in Homer, so where are you from?" asked Maggie.

"My family is from Naknet," said Hanta. "It's a little town north of the Alaskan Peninsula on the Naknet River. It runs from Naknet Lake to the Bearing Sea. Our ancestors fished salmon on that river."

"Why did you leave?"

"It was because of my wife."

"You were married?"

"Yes," said Hanta as he smiled wistfully into the ocean. Then he turned to her. "Anka was much like you—a rebel, a non-conformist."

"Ha! That's me all right. What happened?"

"We were part of an arranged marriage, which is an old Inuit custom. I was nineteen and Anka was eighteen. Anka's name means goddess of fertility and childbirth, which my family thought was a good sign…but it turned into an ironic tragedy."

Hanta plugged in the coordinates for the fishing grounds, set the boat on autopilot, and turned his attention to Maggie. "Having children is very important to our people, and Anka became pregnant shortly after we were married. The Inuit have a tradition called *pittailiniq*. It's a set of rules that pregnant women are expected to follow in order to have a successful delivery."

"What kind of rules?"

"Oh, let's see…It's taboo to walk backward or the baby will come breech. If you take naps or lay around too much, the delivery will take too long. Always work fast and complete every project quickly, or the delivery will take too long. Don't wear tight pants or you will have a hard delivery. Don't scratch your stomach or you'll get stretch marks."

"For God's sake," interrupted Maggie. "That's bunch of old wife's tales."

"Of course, it is," said Hanta, "and that's what Anka believed too. She didn't follow any of the rules or taboos while she was pregnant—and the whole community knew it."

Hanta ran a hand through his hair. "Whenever an old woman from the tribe would reprimand her for one thing or another, Anka would just shrug and walk away."

"That sounds like what I would do," said Maggie, "but I'd probably add a few colorful expletives."

Hanta smiled but continued. "Then Anka went into labor. We called the midwife—which is also our custom. It's very rare for a doctor to be present—and there are few hospitals anyway." Hanta swallowed hard. "I could not be present for the birth, so I had to remain outside her room. All I could do was listen to Anka scream. It took more than twenty-four hours for her to deliver our son—and he was stillborn."

"Oh, how terrible," said Maggie. She reached for Hanta's shoulders and hugged him tightly. "What happened to Anka?"

"I sat with her right after the baby was born. She was exhausted and could barely speak. She kept whispering how sorry she was for not being a better wife and not following *pittailiniq*. I told her that was silly, and that it wasn't her fault."

Hanta wiped a tear from his eye. "Anka died the following day. They said she bled to death. Just before she died, she said, 'Find another woman, Hanta—one who is better than I am.' I told her that the reason I loved her was because she was not like the others."

Hanta looked ahead to the Gulf of Alaska. "That was ten years ago. Everyone in the community blamed her for losing our child."

"How unfair," said Maggie. "Women are always to blame."

"That's usually not the case for Inuit women," said Hanta. "Men treat women as equal partners—and it's important that we have a partner. In the old days, it was impossible to survive without a spouse to share the work. The men hunted and fished while the women butchered the animals, skinned the hides, and prepared the food."

"You should see me filet a walleye," said Maggie. "Gimme a sharp knife and thirty seconds, and I'll give you two boneless fillets."

Hanta laughed. "You would have been highly respected in our village."

"But you didn't get re-married after you lost Anka?"

"That was another problem for me. My family proposed many suitable women for me to marry but Anka spoiled me. None of those women made me feel the same way she did. It wasn't long before I was accused of being arrogant. 'You think you're too good for us. You're a snob. Can't you be happy with a traditional wife?' Finally, I had enough. I decided to leave and move to Homer where I could still fish, but not in the old ways."

"I know about family pressure," said Maggie as she squeezed Hanta's hand. "I hope you find what you are looking for,"

Hanta squeezed her hand in return and said, "There is an Inuit proverb that says, 'I will endure the darkness because it shows me the stars.'"

"I love stargazing," said Maggie. "The sky over Lake Superior was beautiful."

Later that night when the sun finally sank below the summer horizon, Maggie and Hanta lay together on the roof above the wheelhouse. They searched for that rare star that appears briefly in the summer sky.

"There it is," said Maggie. She turned to Hanta. "I know an Inuit proverb too."

"What proverb is that?"

"May you have kindness in your heart and a plump woman in your furs."

Beth

The hold of the *Red Tempest* was full of Coho salmon. It was late September, and the boat was returning to Homer at the end of the fishing season. Hanta was in the captain's chair. Bert was on the radio coordinating the delivery of their catch, and Max was taking a nap in his berth below deck. Beth and Maggie sat on the deck sipping double espressos.

"I'm getting hooked on this coffee of yours," said Maggie, "and I don't even need a shot of Jim Beam for flavoring." She held the espresso cup in the air. "But I still like the feel of a good, old-fashioned mug. Can't get a grip on this little thing."

"Next time I'll make you an Americano," laughed Beth.

"How's the book coming?" asked Maggie. "Does the caffeine help your writing?"

"The coffee keeps me going," said Beth, "but I came to Alaska to find inspiration. So far, I've failed." She sipped her espresso reflectively. "I'm still struggling to find a worthy man for my hero in *Lady Candue Meets Her Match*. My readers—nearly all are women—have certain expectations. They tolerate a hero who is arrogant and vain—matter of fact, they expect him to be handsome and conceited—but at the end of the day, by the time he rescues the damsel in distress and gets her into bed, the damsel has to feel good about it."

"Dick made me feel that way when I first met him," said Maggie, "but at the end, he made me feel like shit."

"Exactly," said Beth. "Your Captain Dick showed promise—I thought he'd be the perfect prototype for my character, but after that first fishing expedition—what a disappointment. I couldn't write a guy like that into my story—maybe he can be the villain in another book."

"He sure was a disappointment to me too," said Maggie.

Maggie shook her head and thought for a moment. "What about Max? He's handsome and arrogant."

"Hmm. Too nerdy," said Beth. "Who thinks of an accountant as a love interest? I'll bet as a kid he went to bed playing with his slide rule."

"Of the people you've met in Homer," said Maggie, "that leaves Bert and Hanta."

"Bert's entertaining, but he's a nerd like Max—and he looks like a toad…Don't ell him that. He'd be devastated."

"I don't think so," said Maggie. "He'd think it's funny. What about Hanta, then?"

Maggie paused to consider her next remark. "I think I'm in love with him."

Beth looked startled. "You sure he's not another of your impulsive infatuations?"

"I don't think so. He might be the real McCoy."

"Good for you, Maggie," said Beth. "Hanta's a good man. But you've read my books. Hanta doesn't belong in that crowd. My heroes are handsome, tough guys who always save the girl, but they're selfish—just looking for sex—until they discover how they must change to find true love. It's what my readers expect. Anything less, and the book wouldn't sell."

"Your books sure have succeeded so far," said Maggie. "I used to dream about your characters." She sighed. "Those guys were my idols—until I met Hanta."

"Thanks Maggie. I guess that's the goal of all romance writers."

Beth paused and thought for a moment. "Maybe that's my problem, Maggie. Maybe I'm tired of the same old ending. Maybe I'm perpetuating a myth that's unattainable…but I don't know if I have the guts to break the old mold—to change the stereotype—to risk disappointing my readers."

"Who cares?" said Maggie. "Your fans are loyal. They'll buy the book regardless of who is the hero. Maybe you can persuade women to start dreaming of a different kind of guy."

"Maybe you're right."

Max

After unloading their catch, Hanta pulled the *Red Tempest* within sight of the dock in Homer.

"There are two guys in dark suits standing on our dock," he shouted, "and I don't think they're looking to buy fish."

Max popped his head out of the cabin and squinted through the morning mist. "Damn. I suppose they're looking for me."

Bert had been looking through his binoculars and draped them around his neck. He called to Max, "They're looking right at us. The short one is looking back at me with his binoculars and the other guy is holding a briefcase."

"Let me take a look," said Max.

He took a long look before handing them back to Bert. "It's gotta be the feds—IRS, FBI. Who knows? I wonder how they tracked me down."

Max turned to Maggie and Beth who were standing on the deck with him. "Well guys, the last six weeks have been a little slice of heaven. Rowdy Limburg's had the time of his life."

"You've been a good deck hand," said Bert. "We couldn't have had a successful fishing trip without you."

"I think Rowdy caught on to fishing for salmon faster'n I did," said Maggie, laughing. "And he didn't get seasick."

"Your stomach behaved itself pretty well," said Beth.

"Thanks to your good cookin'," said Maggie.

"Max, should I turn around and head back out to sea?" asked Hanta.

"Naw," said Max. "Too late now. May as well face the music. If I gotta go to prison, I may as well get started."

Hanta drove the Tempest next to the dock, and Bert and Maggie stepped off the boat. Bert secured the bow mooring line to a cleat and Maggie tied off the stern.

"We're looking for a Maxwell Wharton," said the man carrying the briefcase. "He's wanted in Minnesota."

Maggie approached the shorter of the two and looked down at him. "Who wants to know?" she demanded.

"Our employer sent us," he said. "We've been looking for Max for a couple of months now. His son, Clyde suggested we try up here. He gave us an address with a post office box number. Clyde said that Max gave him the address so that he could send him the proceeds from the sale of his house in Minnesota."

"That so?" said Maggie. "No Max on this boat."

"You sure? We did a little snooping around town," said the man with the briefcase. "When we showed a picture of Max to the post office agent, he told us he looked a lot like a man named Rowdy Limburg."

"You got a Rowdy Limburg on board?" said the short one.

"I'm Rowdy Limburg," interrupted Max. He stepped off the boat and onto the dock, "And I'm also Max Wharton. Am I under arrest?"

"Under arrest?" said the man with the briefcase. "For what? Of course not."

"What then?" said Max. "Who are you?"

The short one extended his hand to Max. "I'm Ted and this is Roy. We represent *Axel and Sons*. Mr. Axel told us to find you and not to return until we did. He wants to re-hire you."

Max returned a tentative hand to Ted and then to Roy. "I must say that I'm relieved. I thought you were someone else."

Max watched a couple of gulls fight over a dead minnow that had been left on the dock. "I don't want to return to Minnesota," he said. "I'm happy here in Alaska."

"Yes. That's fine," said Roy, "but the last time *Axel and Sons* hired a different accounting firm, they made an absolute mess of things. Mr. Axel wants you to work your financial magic and file this year's return."

Max gestured toward the boat next to them. "The last six weeks I've been a deck hand on the *Red Tempest*, and it's been the best six weeks of my life."

"Do you have an internet connection in this godforsaken place?" said Ted as he swatted a mosquito. "You can work remotely. The company will fly you to Minnesota a couple of times a year when you're needed in person."

"Remember that the winters are pretty long in Alaska," warned Roy. "You'll need something to do. You could fish in the summer and work for us in the winter."

"I don't know," said Max.

Roy pulled a sheaf of papers from his briefcase. "Why don't you look this over. It's a contract. You can write your own ticket."

Max accepted the document. "You guys drive a hard bargain," he said.

"You'll notice," said Ted, "that there won't be any more year-end bonuses. Figure that in when you're making your offer."

Max laughed. "That's a relief. I'll run this by my attorney, and let you know later this week."

"We've seen all we need to see in Homer," said Roy. "The sooner, the better."

When Ted and Roy returned to their hotel, Max turned to the *Red Tempest* crew. "Do you think that would work—to fish in the summer and work as an accountant in the winter?"

"Sure would," said Bert. "Lots of fishermen take part-time jobs in the winter—if they can find them."

"Will you have an opening for a deck hand next year?" asked Max.

"We still need to secure financing for our partnership," said Hanta. "Without that, we won't have a boat."

"I believe I can help you there too," said Max, "—assuming you're still looking for another partner."

"Welcome aboard the *Red Tempest* partnership, Max."

Chapter 24
Epilogue

Linda

It took Linda three months to go broke—a feat that most high rollers would be proud of. She gambled away the $75,000 from Max's savings account, the proceeds from the sale of their home, and the remainder of the nest egg from her parents. She was left with Clint and her trim physique. Clint used his contacts as a porn-star recruiter to sign Linda and him to a multi-year contract with AARP. They moved to Los Angeles and became successful stars in sex videos for seniors.

Max

Axel and Sons were not the only ones to discover that Max had fled to Homer, Alaska. The IRS also tracked him down. The government had received the offshore voluntary disclosure document written by Max's attorney, Frankie Hillsborough. Max agreed to pay the back taxes, interest, and penalties on the portion of bonuses that Frankie had left in the Swiss bank account. But since the letter was tardy and Max wanted to avoid serving time, he negotiated a plea bargain with the IRS agents. Max offered information about Phil and his Whitefish coke ring in return for a clean record—one that cleared him of any charges that would have stained his reputation.

Clyde

Clyde was evicted from the Wharton's home in Minnesota after it was sold, but he was thrilled with the windfall from its sale. He moved to Whitefish, Montana and became a ski bum, fulfilling his father's greatest dream. He found lodging in a small log cabin near the end of a cul de sac. For once in his life, he took his father's advice and tried to choose his friends and lovers carefully. Phil did not pose a problem for Clyde because Phil was on his way to the penitentiary. Twila did not pose a problem for Clyde because Twila was on her way to treatment for the fourth time. Jake, however, *did* pose a problem for Clyde because Jake became the new local drug dealer. Clyde happily accepted Jake's free drinks and a position as bookkeeper for the *Hellroaring Saloon*.

Clyde never met his biological father since Clint and Linda remained in Los Angeles and never returned to Whitefish.

Maggie

Maggie filled the long Alaskan winter nights in Hanta's arms. She skipped her regular visits to the pharmacy and became pregnant a month later. She successfully delivered their son without following any of the taboos of *pittailiniq*. The boy had bright red hair—a novelty in the Inuit community. They named him Kissimi because of his independent spirit.

Beth

Lance Freeport re-wrote *Lady Candue Meets Her Match* using Hanta as the hero's prototype. Beth's fans loved the book but were heartbroken to learn that it would be the last of the *Lady Candue* series.

In the quiet evenings on the *Red Tempest*, Beth had listened to Max's account of his misadventures with the IRS. She became inspired to write a new book called *The Injustice*. Her protagonist, Rowdy Limburg was not as lucky as Max had been. He fought a losing battle against what he thought were the injustices of FATCA (The Foreign Account Tax Compliance Act) and spent ten years in prison. The book found a sympathetic audience with the political right and became a best seller after it was discovered by Fox News. Rowdy became a cult hero, martyred for his stance against federal government interference.

Acknowledgements

Special thanks to Holly Neaton and her family for guidance about purse seine fishing in Alaska, to Wayne Pike and Doug Schmidt for their editing assistance, and to Patty Nelson for her help in designing the cover.

ABOUT THE AUTHOR

Dave Wright is a retired veterinarian from Buffalo, Minnesota. His goal in communication, whether in public speaking or writing, is to engage and entertain his audience. Dave and his wife, Sue, have two sons and five grandchildren.

Also, by Dave Wright:

"Oh, It's You: The Extraordinary Life of a Veterinarian"

Find more of his essays and short stories at his blog:

www.davewrightwrites.com

Made in the USA
Monee, IL
22 August 2023

41451844R00075